A NAUGHTY TALE FROM DORSET

Abigail Roberts

authorHOUSE®

AuthorHouse™ UK Ltd.
1663 Liberty Drive
Bloomington, IN 47403 USA
www.authorhouse.co.uk
Phone: 0800.197.4150

Published by AuthorHouse   08/18/2014

ISBN: 978-1-4969-8715-0 (sc)
ISBN: 978-1-4969-8716-7 (e)

I dedicate this book to my Mum who
I miss with all my heart x

John 8:2-1 English Standard Version (ESV)² Early in the morning he came again to the temple. All the people came to him, and he sat down and taught them. The scribes and the Pharisees brought a woman who had been caught in adultery, and placing her in the midst ⁴they said to him, "Teacher, this woman has been caught in the act of adultery. ⁵Now in the Law Moses commanded us to stone such women. So what do you say?" ⁶This they said to test him that they might have some charge to bring against him. Jesus bent down and wrote with his finger on the ground. ⁷And as they continued to ask him, he stood up and said to them, "Let him who is without sin among you be the first to throw a stone at her." ⁸And once more he bent down and wrote on the ground. ⁹But when they heard it, they went away one by one, beginning with the older ones, and Jesus was left alone with the woman standing before him. ¹⁰Jesus stood up and said to her, "Woman, where are they? Has no one condemned you?" ¹¹She said, "No one, Lord." And Jesus said, "Neither do I condemn you; go, and from now on sin no more."]]

The names in this book have been changed to protect the innocent, and the downright naughty

ABOUT THE AUTHOR

Hello, my name is Abigail. I'm now fifty years old and emigrated from a sleepy Dorset town to the Costa del Sol in June 2013. I am a mother to four children and have been married three times. I had hoped to marry for life to my first husband at the age of twenty years old, but it didn't turn out that way. The same goes for my second and third marriages. I wasn't a perfect wife by any means, but I really have tried my best. The phrase "all give and no take" is very apt in my case—with me doing all the giving. I am currently separated from husband number 3 and am very happy to be single again. They say life begins at fifty, and it is true in my case.

The following story is my personal account of how I went from being a stay-at-home mum to getting involved in the swinging scene, which then led to me working as an independent escort in 2010 when I was forty-six years old. All my life, I have sought approval, whether it be from my mother or my husbands, and I'm now happy just to be able to be me and not have to answer to anyone. When you reach the end of my book, I wonder what you will think of me. Will you think I'm a bad person or perhaps someone you could get on with, if you met me? I started writing my story when I was at a very low ebb, and it gave me something positive to focus on. I've heard people say that it's a good thing to get your thoughts and feelings down on paper, and I do feel better for having written it.

INTRODUCTION

I remember my Mum telling me about three years ago, that I should write a book as I've had what I suppose, you could call a colourful life (it certainly hasn't been dull) and she seemed to think I'm the type of person that could write a good story.... and this was before I told her I was doing escort work. I'd always felt I could tell my Mum anything and telling her about my new 'job' was no exception. Her reaction to that little bit of news? She just looked at me, sighed and said "it's pointless me trying to talk you out of it because you've never taken my advice anyway... but for God's sake Abigail, do be careful and if you do ever write a book, please wait until I'm 6feet under." Sadly she passed away last year from a prolonged illness. If she's looking down on me from somewhere, I know she will be happy I've tried my hand at writing, but shaking her head at the content of the book! Many changes have happened in my life since she died, and at the moment I'm at a crossroads, not sure which way to turn. (We'll get to that a bit later) It occurred to me recently that now might be a good time to write my story as it will give me something to focus on, and take my mind off other things that haven't been going well in my life lately.

CHAPTER 1

I lost my virginity when I was 16 and remember thinking "is that it?" The second time was a bit better and after that there was no stopping me. Let's just say I was very promiscuous. One night stands were a regular occurrence and if I didn't end the night in bed with someone, I'd consider it a bad night. I was a nightmare teenager and drank to excess and experimented with various drugs, including cocaine-which made me feel so ill I never wanted to repeat the experience thank goodness. When I was in my early twenties' I did have a few sessions with a shrink, as I was a bit worried why I behaved like I did and she came to the conclusion that a lot of it was because I craved the attention and affection I lacked as a child. I know, I know, "oh that old chestnut" I hear you say, but that was the conclusion she came to, after my visits to her. I was sent to a boarding school at the age of 8 even though my family home was ten minutes' drive away. I was a full time boarder and I hated it. I was expelled at the age of 15 for sneaking out after lights out, raiding the tuck shop and generally just being rebellious. After the expulsion I was sent to a Comprehensive school which I fit into well as the pupils there were as bad as me! Looking back I realise it was because Mum liked her extended holidays and only having herself to think about that made her send me to Boarding school- having me around would have cramped her style. That realisation as I grew older did hurt me, and for a time Mum and I didn't get on at all (screaming matches and punch ups in shops, the usual kind of mother/teenage daughter thing!) However as I got older, I could understand better the reasons behind the way she was with me, mainly due to her own upbringing. Like me, my Mum was an only child. My maternal grandparents were very intellectual people, my Grandfather was a Professor at Queen Mary College in Cambridge and Granny spent most of her time reading, so my Mum spent most of her younger years left to her own devices until she was sent to boarding school at the age of 9. Mum and I did become closer as the years went on and I was devastated when she became terminally ill. As her illness progressed, we spent time together and built a lot of bridges. I am glad we were able to do this as it has helped me cope with losing her. She once told me she felt unable to show me love and affection as a child because she hadn't received any from her own parents. That really didn't make sense to me because when I started having children of my own, I was a very loving demonstrative Mum. Many times throughout my life I wished I wasn't an only child and felt this especially when she died. I miss her very much and always will. If people enjoy this book, she would be proud of me, but there's no way in the world Id have wanted her to read it!

CHAPTER 2

I'm sorry to say I have 3 failed marriages behind me. I married the first time at the age of 19, to a man called Neil. My first son, Liam, was born when I was 20. Neil was a very charming man and easy going, until he got drunk and he would then become violent and abusive towards me. My mother in law told me that she had been raped by Neil's father and that Neil had been conceived as a result. She was convinced he had 'bad blood' in his veins and this was the reason he was abusive towards me. I would often leave him and take Liam with me, to go and stay with my Mum but would weaken when Neil rang me, begging forgiveness and promising he would never hit me again. It was 6 years before I realised that he was not going to change and when I asked him what it would take for him to leave Liam and I, he looked at me very calmly and said £5.000, and I'm gone'. I told my Mum what he wanted and she was so relieved that he was finally going to leave us in peace, that she gave me the money to give him.-'money well spent' I remember her saying. He moved out and into his Aunts' house. After leaving us, I would go and visit him so that he could see Liam who I believe he really did love but sadly not as much as alcohol. He also struggled with depression-a few years passed and when Liam was 12 years old, I received a call from Neil's

Great Aunt to tell me that Neil had hanged himself in her garden and had been discovered by one of his 3 cousins. I took Liam to his father's funeral and it was a very sad day. The cousin who found him hanging from the tree said that finding Neil like that would stay in his memory forever. Apparently Neil hadn't died quickly, but strangled himself and I was advised by his Mother not to go and visit him in the Chapel of Rest as he looked absolutely awful. Despite the way he had treated me during our marriage I was so upset that he had committed suicide, and in some way I felt guilty because I thought I should have seen the signs that he was so depressed when I took Liam to visit him, and then I would have tried to get him some help. I think now, with hindsight, his death has contributed to Liam's problems which I will tell you more about later on.

CHAPTER 3

When Liam was nearly 7, I met a man called Steven, who was to become my second husband. We had 2 children together, Ben and Lisa. We were married for 14 years but the marriage had been in trouble for the last 5 of those years- I started to feel like a piece of furniture and unwanted. Steven preferred to be in the pub with his friends while I was left bringing up the kids. Ours was a very volatile, love/hate relationship and we had many drunken fights-on one occasion I stabbed him in the head with a car key – a friend of mine asked me afterwards if I was trying to give him keyhole surgery! I had a few flings with other men, not with any intention of committing to them, I think I just craved attention and some affection that was lacking at home. None of these affairs lasted long until I met Andrew. I really believed he was my 'Mr Right' and after a 6 month affair, I told Steven I was leaving him. He threatened to kill me if I took Ben and Lisa with me and leaving them was the hardest thing I've ever done, but I agreed to let them stay with their Dad mainly to keep the peace and also was glad that the children could stay in the home and the schools that they were familiar with. I reassured them both that I would see them regularly which I did.

CHAPTER 4

By this time, Liam was a teenager and in lots of trouble with the police. At the age of 16 he was sentenced to 6months in a young offenders institute for beating a man up, who it later transpired was an ex-policeman which didn't do him any favours when he to court. He has been in and out of prison ever since and at the time of writing this, is currently serving 3 years. I moved into a rented house with Andrew and it was a huge shock to find myself pregnant with his child at the age of 40. I did consider having an abortion but couldn't bring myself to get rid of the baby who was Andrew's 1st child. After living with a traveller who worked when the mood took him, I was happy that I had met a good solid man who worked hard and I thought he would be a good provider and father. Amy was born in 2005-Andrew's family were delighted, as were Ben and Lisa. Liam was in prison at this time and seemed uninterested in his new baby sister. I suffered for the first time in my life with post natal depression and was prescribed anti-depressants by the Doctor. Amy is now nine and I am still taking those tablets simply because I'm now addicted to them and it's so hard trying to come off them. Life went on, with me seeing Ben and Lisa as much as I could, and getting used to becoming a Mum again later in life. I was very happy with Andrew, who was a long distance lorry driver and only home at weekends' He was a very quiet man whereas I'm the complete opposite but we did get along well, although that might not have been the case if he had been coming home from work every day! The subject of marriage never came up which suited me as I was adamant I would never do it again about the first 2 failed attempts.

CHAPTER 5

Everything changed one Friday evening, when after returning from his week away at work, I laid out my naughty undies on our bed which he saw and made the comment "Mm mm, it's so good to be home!" I told him I was going to get in the bath and left him watching television in the lounge. The position of our bathroom was such, that if you looked through the door, you could see along the hallway and part of the lounge. I looked round the bathroom door and was just about to tell him to turn the television down, when I noticed his elbow moving very quickly whilst it was resting on the side of the armchair... I continued looking and realised he was sitting there masturbating –I couldn't believe it... there was I hoping for a night of passion and he preferred to get himself off... and if I hadn't seen him I expect that when we would have gone to bed he would have rejected my amorous advances, turned over and gone to sleep saying he was tired! Well I was furious and old feelings of insecurity and rejection welled up inside me. I leapt out the bath, marched into the lounge... he just managed to tuck himself away in time... and asked him why the hell he would rather do that, than make love to me? He said sorry repeatedly (I'm sure, not because he was, but he was just sorry Id caught him) and I calmed down and we started talking. Well, it turned out that he'd lived a very sheltered life, no one night stands, and the 3 long lasting relationships he'd had, were all with women a lot older than him... I was 6 years older than he was by the way, and I was 45 at this particular time. He felt he'd missed out a lot as far as pulling women was concerned and wished he'd had the chance to do more when he was younger. The three relationships he'd had prior to meeting me, had all been with older women and he said he would have loved to have had a threesome, with two women. This didn't shock me as I know many men think the same! I put our conversation to the back of my mind until an opportunity presented itself.

CHAPTER 6

The opportunity came in the form of an old friend of mine called Katy who I'd known a few years. Katy asked me to go with her to her works do which was being held not far away from where we lived. Andrew stayed at home looking after Amy. During the evening Katy and I talked about a lot of things and the subject of sex came up-as it often does on a girly night out! I told her that Andrew wanted a threesome and to my amazement, Katy said she would be happy to help Andrew's dream come true! She and I had both had a fiddle with other women previously, and feeling brave, after a few ciders, I suggested we go back to my place and jump on him. We made our way home, giggling like a pair of schoolgirls as we walked up the road. It did cross my mind to ring Andrew and tell him what we were planning to do, but then I thought no, it will nice to surprise him! It was all very quiet in my flat as we went in, so we crept to my bedroom and opened the door, It was pitch black in the room and I quickly flicked the light on and said 'Move over big boy, we're getting in' Well, he sat up in bed, rubbing his eyes and looking absolutely stunned-hardly surprising really! Katy and I stood at the end of my bed and got out of our clothes as quickly as we could-no finesse at all, given the amount of cider we'd consumed. Andrew still looked completely gobsmacked and seemed to have lost his voice. I pushed Katy round one side of the bed and told Andrew to move over to the middle. I then climbed in on the other side of him so that he ended up sandwiched between us two big ladies! Well, all I can tell you is Katy and I did our best to tease and please him and although he did show willing by kissing us both and having a little fondle with each of us, ''Mr Winky' was showing no sign of wanting to participate and we gave up in the end!! I felt sorry for Andrew as he was so embarrassed and very apologetic but we laughed it off and told him not to worry about it. Katy got out of the bed and said she had better be getting home and that was the end of that. After she left, Andrew and I talked and he said he couldn't believe he wasn't able to get a hard on, and I pointed out that sometimes the fantasy is better than the reality.

CHAPTER 7

The episode wasn't mentioned again and a few weeks went by before he piped up,

'Abby, shall we give swinging a go'

'What?'

'I was thinking it might be good to go and have a look at what goes on in these swinging clubs'

'Andrew, I'm not being funny but you didn't enjoy the threesome we had, what you going to be like when you see lots of people at it in front of you?'

'I just think it's not so personal if there's a lot of people there and you only have to join in if you want to-we could just stand and watch everyone, he replied' I was happy with the idea of spicing up our love life if it was what he wanted, and we started doing some research on the internet....

We discovered there was a swinging club about half an hour drive from our home which surprised us as the area the place was situated was known to be inhabited by middle aged and older middle class folks. On the clubs website it said they have several caravans on their land for people who wished to stay overnight so we booked one for ourselves so that we could have a few drinks and not have to drive home afterwards. We were both so nervous, while we were getting ready at home to go to the party. We didn't know what to wear and In the end Andrew dressed in trousers and short sleeved shirt while I basically went in clothing that might as well have included a chastity belt... I had a pretty good idea what was going to be happening at this club, but had no intention whatsoever of participating in any way. We drove to the club, parked up and Andrew turned to me and said

'I don't think I can do this Abigail'

'I'm nervous too but we're here now, shall we just go on in there and see what it's like? If we don't like it, we'll just go home', I replied. Andrew agreed, and clutching his' Dutch courage'-a bottle of Jack Daniels,' we made our way to the club entrance. Well, when we walked through the door that first time, I looked around, my mouth opened in amazement and I felt like I'd died and gone to heaven. I looked at Andrew and he was standing there looking like his feet had stuck to the floor (by the end of the night they might well have been, body fluids, alcohol and all sorts of other delights spilling everywhere). I noticed he had gone a funny shade of pale and looked absolutely terrified! I persuaded him to move his feet and the club owner who was a lovely lady called Felicity, came over, welcomed us warmly, gave us a much needed drink and offered to give us the guided tour.

CHAPTER 8

The club consisted of a main room when you went in which had a huge red leather bed at one end, a dance pole, lots of comfy seats and sofas. There was a bar, a television playing a porn movie in one corner and I've never seen so much naked and near naked flesh in one place. There was a corridor with 2 very dark playrooms leading from it, and at the far end, a Jacuzzi room. People were sitting around chatting, drinking and all enjoying themselves and each other in every way possible. It was all fascinating to see and I knew I was going to have a good time. Not so Andrew, who spent that evening getting absolutely legless, had no fun with anyone and ended up in our caravan by about 11.30 pm fast asleep... but I didn't. I got drunk and before I knew it, I was in one of the playrooms having the time of my life, participating in one on one and some group sex with guys and women. A combination of a few ciders, the musky smell of sex, and noise of people in the throes of passion was absolutely fantastic and I loved it all. I couldn't believe I was there taking part in everything that was going on. It all felt surreal. It wasn't easy removing all the clothes I'd worn, but with a bit of help, my garments were on the floor in no time and I vowed to myself next time I went there that I'd be wearing a lot less!! I I had full sex with a couple of men in one of the dark playrooms and received oral sex from another man while his partner played with my boobs. Many people were standing around watching what was going on. By the end of the night I sat with a few of the other swingers chatting about our families and other normal stuff and it felt strange but exciting, looking at some of the men and wondering if I had just had sex with any of them! One young couple who were there told me they had booked one of the caravans for a week and that they were there on their honeymoon! The wife told me that the week at the club was a wedding present from her to her new husband-I was amazed to say the least!

I never did confess to my fella all that I'd done that 1st night, I told him I was just watching everyone else and having a few drinks... I felt guilty for having fun without him as it was meant to be something we'd do together... in my own mind I just blamed the booze for my actions and that eased my guilt!. We went along a couple more times and we both had some fun with other people but Andrew decided the group sex thing wasn't for him and he said he'd be more comfortable in a one to one situation. You have to admit, he was a hard man to please…! Because I did like the swinging scene, I didn't want to lose my new found fun and we agreed to have an open relationship. I'd go to the swinging parties once a fortnight and he would go on dating sites to see if he could find himself a "fuck buddy". And he did, quite a few actually, over a period of time, up and down the country while he was working away, and we seemed quite happy with this new dimension to our relationship.

CHAPTER 9

I really looked forward to the swinging parties which were held every other Saturday evening. People from all walks of life, of all ages and every shape and size imaginable went to the parties. One evening a very large married couple decided to sit on the love seat which was suspended from the ceiling. Well as they positioned themselves into it, he sitting in the seat and her on top facing him, I watched fascinated and wondered how on earth they had both managed to get in it. They swung gently backwards and forwards for a few seconds before an almighty crash drowned out the sound of the music that was playing. The weight of the couple caused the seat to break and fall to the floor with one hell of a bang. This poor couple. People rushed to help them up off the floor and they were so embarrassed, they hurriedly dressed rushed out the club, never to be seen again. Oh how we laughed after they'd gone, it was the talking point of the evening... unkind I know, but at least we kept our faces straight until after they'd left.

During another party, a big commotion could be heard from one of the playrooms down the corridor. A few people rushed to see what was happening (I didn't, I was being kept busy with a couple of men on the leather bed in the main room!) I found out afterwards that a woman had gone absolutely ape shit when she discovered that the two men she'd been having a threesome with, were a father and his son. She was screaming at them for deceiving her and not mentioning that they were related. It was only because someone watching their antics made some comment about it- she was definitely not a happy bunny! Now I thought about that afterwards and asked myself how I would have reacted to the father/son scenario and I really don't know why she went so mad. Everyone in the club was over 21 and I didn't see why she made such a fuss to be honest.

During one of the parties, a woman was engaged in group sex with 3 guys. She bit into one of their cocks so hard, he screamed. An ambulance had to be called and he ended up in hospital and needed stitches. The paramedics were kept outside the club for obvious reasons- and the poor man was taken out to them. I would love to have heard the conversation on the way to the hospital! He was at the club a couple of weeks later though, and there couldn't have been any lasting damage because he appeared to be firing all cylinders when I saw him! The "biter" was asked to leave the club and wasn't allowed back in-the male club members were relieved to say the least!

One evening, a fight nearly broke out in one of the playrooms. You may or may not have heard of 'snowballing' It's where a woman (or a man in some cases) gives a man a blowjob. When the man ejaculates into the other persons' mouth, they then pass the sperm into someone else's mouth to swallow. It makes me feel queasy thinking about it (by the end of this book you will probably wonder why) Anyway, the guy who the sperm originally belonged to was angry that his sperm had been passed to someone else, the whole episode nearly resulted in fisticuffs and the people concerned were asked to leave... it sounds and is crazy but such is the swinging scene!

One of the best days at the club was their midweek "cd TV and bi days (and we're not talking electrical' here!). I did love those afternoons and went when I was able to. It was a gathering of anything up to 100 people, mainly transvestites, though everyone was welcome to go along, whatever their sexual preferences. I loved to watch them playing and having sex with each other, though I didn't interact with them myself. I had many an interesting chat with some of them. Many of them said they loved being able to go somewhere and just be how they wanted to be without the need to hide. A lot of them had the most beautiful clothing, designer stuff and shoes to die for. It made me smile seeing them with their make up on and trying to look as feminine as possible when their Adam's apples were bobbing up and down! They'd bring along lots of different toys and whips and regular thrashings were given to anyone who fancied it! One of the not such fun parts of those afternoons (particularly for Felicity) was that occasionally there would be faeces over the floor in the gents' loos. This apparently was caused by too much vigorous anal activity which weakened the bowels. Felicity could often be seen with mop and bucket in hand heading to the loos to clean the mess, whilst swearing under her breath.

I did enjoy the swinging scene and admit I did miss it when I eventually gave it up. It wasn't' just the sexual side of it that appealed to me, I liked the social side of it too, just being able to feel comfortable with people and enjoy a few drinks and share some laughs. Another bonus was that because the club was actually a converted barn on the owners land, the smokers amongst us could sit and have a cigarette without having to stand outside. As you can imagine, there were many real characters there. One of whom I will call Gill. Gill was a bubbly middle aged lady whose voice was similar to mine. Deep and gravelly- (fag related) with a voice that fit that of a farmers' wife. On one occasion she came to the club holding a lead. On the end of the lead was a blond haired young man in his mid-twenties with a black and silver studded collar around his neck. He seemed perfectly happy to be bought in like that and she took him to the middle of the main room and chained him up naked to the dance pole for the duration of her stay, until she decided it was time to go home. The first time I witnessed this, I said to her, "Gill, how can you be so mean to him like that?" She replied that he loved being treated like it and told me to go and ask him myself if I didn't believe her. As I approached him he looked very downcast, and not like he was enjoying himself at all.

"Are you alright, do you want a drink or something?" I asked him. He didn't even look up at me but replied

"No thank you, my mistress will punish me if I eat or drink anything" I looked over at Gill who was watching our exchange with a beady eye. I felt so sorry for him until after about 4 hours he shouted across the room, "Mistress, may I go to the toilet please?" Gills response to that was to march over to him screaming "did I say you could speak?"

"No mistress, sorry mistress I'm very sorry" She then unchained him from the pole, got her whip out and thrashed his bare bum with it... I had never seen that done to anyone before, and was watching transfixed until about 3 minutes after the whipping began he ejaculated all over the floor! I couldn't believe it. Seems he really did enjoy it after all and there was I, worrying about him!

Another practise that used to go on was Bukkake. A very messy business that some of you might have heard of. For those of you that haven't, it involves a female laying down on a bed or table, surrounded by several men. The men will ejaculate all over her... a "good" Bukkake session is defined by whether the men are able to all cum at the same time over the person. This isn't something that I ever wanted to volunteer for but I didn't mind watching! I did find it very erotic if it had been a successful session but also amusing watching about 8 men trying their hardest to orgasm at the same time...concentration etched on every face!

One of the swingers I became friendly with was a lady called Anna. She lived with 2 guys who catered to her every whim, sexual and everything in general. One of the men was her husband 'I'm guessing in his early 60s and the other man who I will call Ian. They were all dedicated swingers and seemed very happy with their arrangement. A buffet was provided at every party and included venison for anyone who wanted it. Anna once told me there was nothing she loved more than putting a freshly killed animals blood all over her body, she found it a real turn on. I had my own thoughts about it but kept them to myself. It's no good being judgemental when you're part of the swinging scene! I will never forget Ian... after my first sexual encounter with him, he stood up adjusted himself and said "thank you my darling, you've just made an old man very happy" I stared at him and in the next to no lighting of the playroom I was struggling to guess his age, though I would have guessed he was in his early 60s. I said "how old are you then?" "79" was his reply. Well, I was mortified to learn that I'd just had sex with a man of that age-I couldn't believe it! Trust me when I tell you he didn't let his age slow him down and knew how to please the ladies! His favourite party outfit was a pink tutu and he'd strut around wearing that, much to every ones amusement!

Another swinger I became friends with and still keep in touch with was a very wealthy business man called Jason, who was in his early 50 s. We would meet up at the club on party nights as we lived a long distance from each other. Usually we would share one of the clubs caravans for the night. Believe it or not, he and I never once had sex with each other, though he didn't mind me jumping in his bed the following morning to give him a blow job before he headed home. I think it's because we didn't have sex that we are still friends and have stayed in touch with each other ever since. I was and am still very fond of him. One morning after a party he stepped outside the caravan and shouted back in to me "Abigail is this one of your bras out here? There are cars, planes and all bloody sorts tangled up in it!" I thought that was so funny! If you saw my bras you would understand!

One night I decided to take my tent to the club and sleep in that the night. There was a huge field ideal for camping out the back of the club and people used to take their tents motorhomes or their own caravans if they wanted to stay overnight. I took a camping stove with me and had a coffee before joining the party. I went back to my tent at the end of the evening, drunk as a skunk. I got into the sleeping bag and decided I'd have one more cigarette before going to sleep. I was fumbling about in the darkness trying to find my fags but gave up in the end... which is just as well. In the morning I heard some people outside my tent asking each other if they could smell gas? It was then I realised I hadn't turned the camping stove off properly the night before... good job I couldn't find my fags in the night. I could have blown myself and others to kingdom come, doesn't bear thinking about really. It was fun though camping out. People could be heard in the night and the following morning tent hopping and the sounds of sexual activity would ring out across the field often followed by the heavenly smell of bacon cooking. A lot of the "campers" would get together, have some breakfast and a laugh over anything that had happened the previous evening! All good fun until you hear about marriage break ups which is inevitable in that environment of course. Some of the people I met had been swinging for years, some were new to it and enjoying it at that time, others would go to the club once and never be seen again. Like many things in life, you don't know if it's for you until you try it. Personally I really loved all the new experiences and felt very comfortable with the whole scene. One thing I did find bizarre about the swingers club was that most of the people who went there were insistent on using condoms when they were having sex with each other-and yet they still gave each other oral sex which carries its own risk of sexual diseases-I have to admit I did too.

One of the swingers occasionally held parties at his house. He'd converted his attic into a huge playroom and everyone had a great time up there. He must have had every dildo known to man and womankind. There was a love swing, chains, blindfolds and basically something for everyone whatever you were into. His double ended dildo was a hit amongst ladies wanting to have fun with each other. Most of us would stay overnight as he had plenty of bedrooms to accommodate his guests. It was all good fun and so keen was I to get there one evening, I got stopped for speeding. Absolutely typical that I was wearing next to nothing and looked like the tart I was. I leaned over to try and grab my jacket off the back seat but there was no time. The copper looked me up and down through the window, face expressionless-my face had gone blood red at this point-he then gave me a ticket and after telling me off, he sent me on my way with the words "enjoy your evening" I was pleased to see a twinkle in his eye as he said it and was grateful he was one of the nicer officers, and hadn't made me get out the car!

During a pub lunch with Mum and her friend Veronica one Sunday afternoon, we were having a giggle as I told them about the things that went on at the club and, with a twinkle in my eye, asked Veronica if she would like to come along with me and see it all for herself one day? 'Oh my God no', she replied, in her frightfully posh Joanna Lumley voice, 'I would not want anyone's genitalia flapping around in MY face, thank you very much!' Mum and I roared with laughter! Veronica is a lovely lady, and a childhood friend of my Mum. She was a huge support to my stepdad and I when Mum was nearing the end of her life. She's a lady with a big heart and I thank her for being there for us when we needed her.

CHAPTER 10

As time went on, I became good friends with some of the swinging folks, outside of the club as well as inside. One of them, a lovely lady called Tina, and I went for a coffee in town one day and she said, "Have you ever thought about doing escort work Abigail? It was one of those, "choke on your drink moments"... I spluttered out, "good God no, I couldn't do that-. I like the swinging but I couldn't take money from a man for sex".

'Why not?' she asked, 'I work through a website, I do webcam shows, dirty phone calls as well as the escort work and I'm raking the money in, all tax free'

'I couldn't do it,' I said, 'I haven't got the body for it, or the looks for that matter, I bet most of the women on there are drop dead gorgeous, I can't compete with that'

'Abigail, am I gorgeous looking? I wasn't quite sure how to respond to that as she actually wasn't, but she saved me the embarrassment-'No I'm not, I'm just your average middle aged woman with a body heading south-if I can do it, so can you!'

'Thanks-I think!' We both laughed and she went on to tell me that she could earn £60.00 for half an hour and £100.00 for an hour. It did sound very tempting and she asked me to just have a look at the website at some point to check it all out. She pointed out that as we go to the swingers club and have sex with lots of different people there, why not get paid for it? Hmm, I thought, but that's different isn't it? Anyway, I went home and did have a look at this website. I looked at all the different profiles of the escort workers and noticed- and I don't mean to sound unkind here... that a lot of them didn't look what I would consider "desirable" to the opposite sex. It crossed my mind that if some of them were doing it and making money then maybe I could give it a go. I'm a size 22/24, and as I said earlier, very busty (44f) and a tummy that would best be described as an "apron"... but I thought if I wore my larger lady sexy undies, maybe I could cover all the nasty bits up and be able to attract guys who would be happy to give me some of their hard earned cash. I think I've got an attractive enough face but only when dolled up, and I have been told I "scrub up well"... but then don't we all with a bit of war paint ladies??! After looking at great length at these profiles and arguing with myself whether I should try it or not, I decided to give it a go... The first step would be to set up my own profile and I thought I would start with some webcam work and phone chats, rather than going straight in to the escort side of things-. it wasn't long before I was all set up for business. After looking at other profiles on the website, my profile read something like this-

Hello, I'm Abigail. I'm a mature sexy woman, clothes size 18/20 and natural bust size 44 g. I've been described as 'warm natured, genuine and friendly'. I genuinely enjoy sex, it's not a chore. I like French kissing, lots of foreplay, oral and penetration. If you are into anything that might be considered a little different, that you would like to do with me, then please mention it when you ring me, to save any embarrassment when you arrive! I offer a relaxed service, and if you are nervous about seeing me, please don't be. I don't bite – unless you ask me to! I will do my best to put you at ease. I don't watch the clock and if we're enjoying each other and go a little over the appointment time, who cares? If you want to use the shower/loo when you arrive, just ask. I do like men to be clean and smelling nice when they come to see me and I do the same for you. I will be wearing sexy undies when you arrive, eg Basque, stockings, high heels etcetera but I also have a selection of other sexy outfits and uniforms that you might prefer me to wear, so just let me know! If you are looking for a sexy, sensual encounter with a real woman, please get in touch and I look forward to meeting you!

Now was that written like a true professional or what?! It's so easy to tap away on a keyboard, but the confident image I aimed to portray hid the fact that I was scared stiff and couldn't quite believe what I was embarking on and I was very nervous.

When Andrew came home the following weekend from work, I asked him how he would feel about me doing escort work. He was against the idea to begin with and was concerned that it would affect Amy's upbringing, which I assured him it wouldn't as I would 'work' during her school hours only (how little I knew!). Somewhat reluctantly, and quite understandably so – he gave me the green light to do it.

CHAPTER 11

It took time but after a few days, Id set up my profile
on the site. I used to take my young daughter to school
and then go home ready to do cam and phone sessions.
This was nerve wracking enough to start with, but once
Id overcome the initial embarrassment of rolling around
on my bed with my "toys", moaning at the right times
etcetera, I did actually begin to enjoy it. I liked watching
the guys getting turned on watching me and it was very
satisfying seeing my bank balance rising. Obviously the
longer you're on the cam or phone with the guy, the more
money you earn so the trick was to keep them as interested
as possible! During cam sessions with different guys, some
of them would ask 'do u do escorting?' to which Id reply
"no" but after being asked this frequently, I realised that
this was where the good money could be earned and I
decided one day that I was going to move up to the next
"step."

CHAPTER 12

When I'd made the decision to try my luck at escorting, I went on the internet and bought lots more sexy undies, high heeled shoes, and a selection of sex toys... I had a collection to be proud of, stashed away in what I called my "whore drawer", next to the bed. I realised I would have to get a decent collection of photographs of myself to attract business, so I asked one of my best friends to come to my house and take some very explicit photos of me-she was surprised, but agreed to come over and do the dirty deed. Well, what a laugh we had- both embarrassed as she was obviously seeing more of me than she really wanted to but when we had overcome that we got on with the photo session and some quite decent pictures were the end result. I described myself as honestly as I could on my profile, my age, looks, likes and dislikes, what I was offering and listed what I wasn't prepared to do (anal, water sports or anything painful). I chose what I hoped were the best photos from the ones taken, and uploaded them onto my profile. I thought I would charge the same as Tina did, I adjusted my details to show that I was now offering escort work, added my phone number and waited for the phone to ring....

Within 45 minutes of updating my profile, my new 'work' mobile phone rang-it was a guy wanting more details of my services. I don't think I ever got to meet him but before long my phone was ringing regularly. Mostly guys wanting more info... in time I realised that a lot of what they were asking me, was already on my profile, and they were only ringing for a cheap thrill... I soon got wise to that one- if I heard any heavy breathing in my ear, I told them to book and pay for a phone chat like everyone else and would end the call quickly! While Id answer what the more genuine ones amongst them wanted to know about me, I felt awkward to start with but gradually got used to it and gained confidence. Within two days of my nether regions being splashed across the site, I had a client lined up and we made an arrangement for him to come and visit me at my house. I couldn't believe I'd had my first call so soon.

It's at this point I should tell you something about my home. I lived in an end of terrace house. I had my own drive way big enough for two cars. My house was overlooked by many others near me and to this day it amazes me that no one ever came up to me and asked me who all these men were coming (forgive the pun) and going. But no one ever did. My house was situated in a very quiet town in Dorset, and quite honestly, if it had been discovered what I was doing, I'm sure the villagers would have found some stocks from days gone by, and put me in them!!! I used to have a giggle to myself that I was doing this naughty "work" in the most unlikely of places. But as the saying goes, "who knows what goes on behind closed doors?!" How true that is.

CHAPTER 13

I wish I could tell you something entertaining about my very first client but I can't. What I can tell you is at the time he was due to arrive I was a nervous wreck. I kept telling myself not to be stupid and that I'd had sex with lots of men in my life time, but the money side of things just made it feel so different. Should I offer him a cup of tea when he came in, should I ask him for the money as soon as he arrived, would he want the loo, would he want me to undress him, and just, well, could I really do this at all? When the doorbell rang I nearly shot out my shoes! I was dressed, I hoped, to kill, in Basque, stockings suspenders and high heel shoes, and even though I'm a big lady I think I looked the part. (this outfit became my standard work attire) I made my way to the front door. Upon opening it, I looked at this pleasant looking middle aged guy who smiled at me. Before he could open his mouth I blurted out "You're my 1st one, I'm so nervous!" how professional... NOT. He was very sweet and just said "are you going to let me in or shall we conduct our business on the doorstep?", so I quickly told him to come in, whilst peeping outside to see if anyone was watching. I managed to compose myself and asked him if he would like a drink, to which he refused and I asked him to follow me upstairs which he did. As soon as we got into my bedroom, he pulled his wallet out his pocket and asked if we could "get this bit out the way"... I nodded and watched, transfixed, as he took three twenty pound notes out and put them on my dressing table. I picked out a condom and gave it to him to put on-my hands were shaking so much I wouldn't have been able to put it on him (I had every colour, flavour and size imaginable-I'd get my friends to pick me some up every time they went to Pound land!), then we proceeded to have just straight sex, no oral, very simple and easy. I soon lost my nerves when it became obvious he was enjoying me, which worked wonders and I found myself responding quite effortlessly to him. I was keeping an eye on the wall clock and remembering what Tina had told me not to go over the agreed appointment time. The half hour went quickly and off went my first satisfied customer! After seeing him out, I went back upstairs and picked up the money he'd left me and I thought how easy it had been to earn it. I assumed (wrongly) that any future clients would be as easy and undemanding- and I found myself looking forward to my next encounter.

CHAPTER 14

My daily routine was mainly as follows... take my daughter to school, come home, shower, and dress up when I was expecting a client. Sometimes whilst I was waiting, I would do some cam or phone work to kill the time. I started the escort work with one client a day, either an hour or half hour appointment, but it wasn't long before I was in demand (much to my pleasant surprise) and then things started going a little crazy. My phone never stopped ringing, morning noon and night. Some days I would see one client, other days I might have three. I seemed to spend most of my life either in the shower or on my bed-I never let clients under the duvet-some sex workers don't allow kissing, we're all different in what we feel acceptable or not. Personally I did like to kiss my clients, which surprised and pleased a lot of them. The one good thing about escort work is that, being an independent escort you can please yourself when you want to work and I did take days off when I needed to give my body a rest. Occasionally I did get sore down below and salt baths helped sooth my parts! Looking back now, I realise that the escort work did take over my life as there came a point when there was little time for anything else, my choice of course, I didn't have to do it, but it all became addictive in a strange way. The money I was earning was great and I knew I could have worked say, 3 days a week and 4 off but I didn't. Looking back now, I realise that I put my friends on the back burner but luckily the ones that mattered most, knew what I was doing and were understanding about it. Many of my clients became regulars which was nice in one way because I knew what they wanted and wouldn't be in for any nasty shocks... but on the other hand some of them were cheeky, for example, one guy said to me,

"I've seen you a few times now, couldn't you give me a discount?"

'I expect you do your shopping at the same supermarket every week, but you don't get a discount when you're paying for it do you?!' I replied. And that was the end of THAT conversation. Most of the guys who visited me said they were married and just not getting enough sex indoors, sometimes due to their wives going through the change of life and losing their sex drive, while some guys told me their wives had various illnesses and were unable to have sex anymore; whether they were telling me the truth or not I can't say but I admit in my strange little mind it kind of made me justify what I was doing with them. Many men said they weren't going without at home, but just liked the thrill of visiting a prostitute... I hate that word but when we get down to the nitty gritty it's what I was. I preferred to think of myself as a very naughty actress. It was my job to make each client I entertained, feel like he was the best lover on the planet. One guy used to take me from behind and shout at me, 'tell me I'm the best shag you've ever had babe', whilst thrusting hard and fast into me – I obliged, and shouted back 'Oh God, yeah go on, do it harder do it harder, you're the best, you're the best!' When I was really thinking, 'bloody hurry up and finish so I can get my face out of this pillow before I suffocate!' I faked so many orgasms during those two years you wouldn't believe. In my mind, I was working, and there to give pleasure, not receive it. Occasionally a client might surprise me and I would have a genuine, knicker exploding climax, but they were few and far between! I was fortunate enough that during those naughty 2 years, that I didn't have any nasty experiences, none of them did anything against my wishes and none of them hurt me. Generally, I can say that I became quite fond of some of them, I could have a laugh and sometimes I got the feeling that they were genuinely happy to have me to chat to. As time went on one guy who came to see me regularly, asked me to give up the job, suggesting I ditch my partner and trade it for a life with them. Promises of being "treated like a queen" didn't tempt me and in the end I had to ask him not to come and see me again which I did feel bad about as I had become quite fond of him, but I had to remain professional or my escort life would have come to an end which I didn't want as I was enjoying it too much. Many of my clients used to say things like-.you're a tart with a heart", or like' the girl next door"- some guys said I was too nice to be in that line of work, while others said I was made for it, opinions varied! I've got a close friend who Id meet every afternoon in the school playground (she knew what I was up to) who regularly asked me what my day had been like and had I had any' nice ones'... she's so funny, a very prim and proper type of woman but she loved hearing all about my antics. She pointed out once that I'd always said I'd like to find some sort of job I could do at home which would fit around school hours... and now I had! What did amuse her was when I told her that Id once asked a client to bring me some double a batteries with him for a toy he liked to use on me as the batteries had run out, and he was happy to oblige!

CHAPTER 15

About a month after starting the escorting, I had a call from a very well-spoken man who said he would like an appointment with me for an hour, so we arranged a day and time. When he arrived, he was very well dressed, suit, tie etcetera and he reminded me of your typical government minister type. As with most my clients I told him to follow me upstairs and he said

'I'd prefer to stay downstairs if you don't mind'

'Oh I said, why is that then?'

'I want you to do something special for me' he replied. I suddenly felt butterflies in my stomach wondering what he was going to come out with next, and I said

"Oh right-you didn't mention anything on the phone when we spoke earlier, what is it you want?" I stated on my internet profile that anything that might be considered unusual must be discussed with me on the phone at the time of booking the appointment. He looked a bit awkward and replied,

"I wondered if you would be happy to give me a pony ride." It took me a moment to digest that bit of information and I just burst out laughing, I couldn't help it and said,

"You are joking aren't you, what do you mean?" he looked quite offended and said he was serious and would

I do it if he gave me an extra fifty quid on top of my normal fee? With pound signs in my eyes I thought let's just do it and get it over with. It did occur to me that up to that point in my new 'job', his was the strangest request yet and that I would probably get a few more in the future so I'd better start getting used to it. I got on my knees and off we went around the lounge-me in my naughty undies, him naked sitting on my back. Every so often he would speak to me like you would a horse, words of encouragement to go a little faster etc. He was a big guy, and after twenty minutes my back was killing me but being the true pro, I carried on. I only came to a stop when he said "We must get you a proper saddle mustn't we my darling?" At that point I started laughing, my knees buckled and I ended up flat on the floor with him on my back. He said in a very sulky voice,

'Well that's not meant to happen"

"You're bloody heavy, I feel absolutely ridiculous and I've had enough" I replied.

"I used to see a lady who was happy to give me rides but she's moved away and no one else seems to want to do it for me"

"Well I'm sorry, but it's the 1st time I've done anything like this and it's just not for me" I found myself feeling a little sorry for him as he looked so sad and I had a sudden idea. I told him to get his clothes on and sit on the sofa while I phoned a friend. (He didn't seem to mind me bossing him about). A lady who attended the swingers club frequently, ran a brothel.

Hi Fran" I said, I've got a gentleman here and he's having trouble finding a lady who'd be happy to give him pony rides "Oh hi Abigail, that's no problem, give him my number and ask him to ring me, one of my girls here will be happy to do that for him" I gave him Fran's number and off he went, practically skipping down the road-or maybe it was a trot?! The next time I saw Fran at the club she told me the jockey would go to her place once a week for his "ride" and bought a saddle, bridle and other horsey stuff from an alternative sex website for his "horse" so all's well that ended well. I will never forget carrying him on my back on the lounge floor, just praying id remembered to lock the back door and that my neighbour wouldn't pop in for a cup of sugar.....!

CHAPTER 16

I had a guy come round for an appointment one day and I'd ask him, as I did a lot of them that came to my house to try to look like a workman or business man-anything that wouldn't arouse suspicion If any curtains were twitching in the vicinity. And living in such a little town where everyone knows everyone, as well as each other's business, this was a strong possibility. Well this middle aged jolly looking chap turned up with a tray of 12 pasties in his hands, 'I thought you might like these" he said.

"Oh lovely, thank you" I replied. He then put the tray of pasties in the kitchen and we went upstairs. Nothing out of the ordinary to report during that particular session, other than him smelling strongly of flour, and when the half hour was over, we came back downstairs. I suddenly realised he hadn't given me my fee "I don't like to ask but you haven't paid me yet". He rummaged through his pockets, got his wallet out looking a bit sheepish said "I hope you won't mind but I'm £20.00 short, but I did bring you the Cornish pasties!'-well what could I do? I told him if he ever came to see me again (he didn't) that he must bring the full amount. I did laugh about it afterwards that I'd been part paid for my ample charms in pasties and I'm glad to say they were delicious. I also realised I still had a lot to learn about escorting…

CHAPTER 17

What always surprised me was the amount of younger guys who wanted to come and see me. I'd ask them on the phone while the appointment was being arranged, what age they were, as I made it clear on my profile I wouldn't see any guys under 21. When the younger ones turned up on the doorstep I believed they were over 21 and even to this day I really hope they were. I'd look at some of them and ask them why on earth they would want to see an old bird like me when there were so many younger, beautiful girls available. The general reply from them was that they wanted to "see what it's like with an older woman". Id almost feel guilty at leading them to my bed for sex, when really I wanted to kiss them on the cheek, tuck them in and give them a hot chocolate! But oh my goodness, how times have changed... the young guys today certainly know their way around a woman's body, much more so than they did years ago when I was younger. Having two grown up sons myself, it did feel strange having sex with the younger ones but in time I did actually enjoy some of them as they're eager to learn new things-I used to think it was a bit like training a naughty eager puppy! Middle aged men are, in my experience anyway, used to lovemaking in a predictable way, normally sticking to their own tried and tested technique which can become quite boring.

One such young guy asked me on the phone one day if I would do some role play with him. He wanted me to be 'Mummy' and told me what he wanted me to do for him. When he turned up I'd say he was mid 20s and a lovely looking guy (if younger ones are your thing). I said to him" you naughty boy, where the hell have you been? you were meant to be home hours ago, get up those stairs and get undressed" I made myself look and sound as angry as I could (there's a lot of acting involved in the escort world and I like to think I became quite adept at it). Off he went, trudging up the stairs and I followed him. For this particular appointment I had to wear thick tights, big knickers, and normal day to day clothes with an apron tied round my waste as he'd requested. When I got in the bedroom he said "Mummy, I'm frightened, 'I've done something naughty and I know you're going to be cross with me." I laid beside him, put his head on my chest (still in my clothes) and after a lot of coaxing, he told me he'd been in my underwear drawer looking at and trying on my pants. I gave him a good telling off (not too loudly in case the neighbours heard), put him over my knee and spanked his bum until it was red, and after that I turned on all fours on the bed while he came all over my bum. When we'd finished and went downstairs I was seeing him out the front door and I said "was that ok for you, did I do it how you like it?" Winking at me he said "it was lovely Mummy, can I come back next week?!!!!" Ah, nothing as satisfying as a happy customer. I saw him on a regular basis after that and I admit I did quite enjoy our little sessions despite my initial misgivings!

CHAPTER 18

You would think that at "that time of the month" I'd be glad of a rest... you'd be wrong. On the website I advertised on, lots of us working ladies (yes, a lot of us are ladies and very hardworking ones at that!) would chat to each other, about our clients or give each other advice on all sorts of escorting issues. Also useful was that women would warn each other which men to avoid if they'd had any unpleasant experiences with them. One trick of the trade I was given was to buy a sea sponge from the chemist. During days I was having a period if I wanted to continue working, I could. Id tear a bit off the sea sponge and insert it into myself, which acted as a plug, preventing the blood flow. I'd be able to work as normal and the guys were none the wiser. I came unstuck one day however, when the sea sponge got wedged too far up inside me after a vigorous hour's appointment with a bank manager, and I had to go to the Doctors and have it removed.' Dare I ask what that is doing up there Abigail?' the Doc asked me. I replied that I'd heard it was a good alternative to tampons... I never used sea sponge again after that. Having said that, one of my clients only wanted to see me when I had my period- he liked me to wear white knickers with the string of the tampon hanging down the side.... he said there was no bigger turn on than being able to be part of a woman's monthly "secret". He was a middle aged man, very attractive, nicely spoken and would bring me flowers and chocolates every time he came to visit, but I never was comfortable with the tampon thing... it was because I genuinely liked him, and his money, that I went along with it, but it's I never really liked doing it.

CHAPTER 19

I will never forget one of the escorts on the website called Leanne who played a trick on me. I was sitting at home one morning, enjoying some peace and quiet and had no intention of doing any appointments this particular day. My phone rang and I was going to ignore it but saw Leanne flash up on the screen, so I answered it.

'Abby' she said, 'couldn't do me a huge favour could you?'

'Yeah sure, what's up?' I replied,

'I've overbooked myself, got two clients due to arrive at the same time-I couldn't send one to you, could I?'

'Is he alright, have you seen him before?' I asked,

'He's a sweetheart, no problem at all' she told me. I really didn't feel like seeing anyone but wanted to help her out so I told her to send him over. I went upstairs, jumped in the shower and got dressed up ready for him. When I heard the doorbell I went and opened the front door. Standing on the doorstep was a middle aged man, in his mid-fifties I would say. He was about five feet five inches tall, stocky build with short brown hair and a much receded hairline. I saw he was holding a large carrier bag with a blue handle sticking out inside it but waited until he was in the hall before I asked him what it was. In a very deep voice he said,

'Hi I'm Malcolm, I'm Leanne's baby' Well….. it isn't often I lose the power of speech but on this occasion, I did. I waited for him to start laughing but he didn't and I realised he was actually serious. It was a jaw dropping moment for me, I can tell you. When I managed to find my voice, I said, 'Leanne's baby?'

'Yes', he replied, 'but she just told me I would have to go to a surrogate Mummy today as she is busy' Now, can you imagine hearing a full grown man saying things like that, and with a totally deadpan expression? It crossed my mind to tell him to bugger off but then the soft side of me came out, with the feeling of needing to please and I heard myself saying in a very gentle voice, 'that's alright, don't worry, I will take care of you'-whilst thinking what a cow Leanne was and what a mouthful I was going to give her when this silly man left. All of a sudden, Malcolm's demeanour changed completely, it was like flicking a switch. He put his thumb in his mouth and said he was hungry so I told him I would feed him when we got upstairs. He held his hand out to me, I took it in mine, took his bag from him, and led him up the stairs, feeling like I was going to my doom and deciding that I really needed a change of profession. Once inside the bedroom, I told him to sit on the bed while I looked in the carrier bag. Inside it was a blue baby changing bag. I pulled it out with him watching me, still sucking his thumb. When I opened the changing bag I could see it contained a baby bottle with milk in, a very large disposable nappy and a pot of nappy rash cream. I had butterflies in my stomach and was as nervous as it was the first time I'd had to do anything like this. I knew this activity was called 'baby minding' and I knew roughly was involved. I really didn't not want to do what was expected of me but professional mode kicked in from somewhere and I thought I must just do it and get it over with.

'Are you ready for your bottle?' I asked him. He somehow managed to give me what I'd describe as a dribbling smile and nodded. 'Come and sit with Mummy then' I said. I then went and laid on my bed, propped up on 3 pillows and patted my legs, indicating that he should come and sit on me. He laid across my lap, I cradled his neck in the crook of my arm and fed him his bottle. It's hard to explain how bizarre it all was. After he had finished his bottle, he sat up and leaned towards me putting his head into my neck and I took that as my cue to burp him. He was silent while I was patting his back. After doing this for about five minutes he said in a babyish voice, 'Malcolm wants nappy on now Mummy' I thought to myself 'Oh my bloody God'. I then pushed him down onto the bed, undid his belt and pulled his trousers down to his ankles, and couldn't fail to notice his erection-dear little thing- He was making strange noises in his throat and had his eyes shut. I then somehow managed to get this enormous nappy under his bum, and kind of crammed his cock into it which wasn't easy. I pulled his trousers back up and did them up as he hadn't told me to do otherwise. He then said to me 'Malcolm wants a cuddle' so I cradled him again on my lap while he gazed up at me and played with my hair. We sat like that for what seemed like ages, with me looking down at his face, and. I just didn't know whether I should be doing something else but assumed as he wasn't talking, that everything was to his liking. All of a sudden he said, 'Malcolm wants to go home now'

'Ok then, off you go' I said. With that, the invisible switch was flicked again and he went back to adult mode.

To my surprise he asked me in his normal voice if he could use my loo, I told him he could and asked him what he was going to do with the nappy he was wearing? He told me he would keep it on until he got back home. He took his wallet out and gave me £100.00, my fee for the hour and after using the loo, we went back downstairs, he kissed me on the cheek at the front door and said 'Bye for now Mummy'-in his normal voice. After he'd gone I poured myself a huge Baileys and rang Leanne.

'You bitch' I said and although I was cross I couldn't keep the smile out of my voice. All I could hear at the other end of the phone was her laughing. I told her to sod off and said I wouldn't fall for any of her tricks again! After a little chat I sat for a while wondering what happens in people's lives to make them want to be treated like that. He didn't want sex and I was grateful for that but it was the most peculiar encounter I ever had with a client, and I knew I would never want to do it again.

CHAPTER 20

Another memorable appointment was with a guy who told me on the phone that he wanted to let himself into my house, I was instructed to leave the front door on the latch.... I was to be laying on my bed with clothes of my choosing on but I must have bare feet. He said he would come up and find me when he arrived- Well I have to say it was the easiest money I've ever earned. I heard him coming up the stairs, I was laying on my bed and following the instructions he'd given me..... I laid there filing my nails. I didn't turn round when he came in the bedroom, just carried on filing. He never said a word and I didn't look at him. He stood at the end of my bed. I heard him remove his trousers and underwear and then he masturbated to climax all over my bare feet. It took eight minutes precisely, when he was done he got dressed, and the only time he spoke while he was in my house was to say "your money's here on the side for you... don't look at me" and off he went back downstairs. I heard the door slam and that was it? It was great to be given £60.00 for doing so little! To my surprise he rang me later in the day and said

"I'm the foot man, just wanted to thank you, it was great" I didn't hear from him again though and was left wondering if he'd have preferred painted toenails?!

Another similar scenario to that one was with a man who told me he wanted me to be standing at my kitchen sink in a short dress, hold up stockings and over the knee high boots when he arrived. Just like the "foot man" he wanted to let himself into my house, find me and he didn't want us to have any conversation at all. I was in position ready for him when he arrived. I heard him come up behind me, I was hoping I might be able to see his reflection in my kitchen window but no such luck! Out the corner of my eye I saw him place 6 £10.00 notes on the worktop. He then pulled my skirt up-I reached round to check he was wearing a condom and then he entered me without making a single noise, even when he had his orgasm. As he was thrusting away behind me I looked out the window and made a mental note to fill the bird feeder in the garden as it was empty. Within 2 minutes of him finishing I heard the front door slam and off he went. I ran to the lounge window in the hope I might see what he looked like as he drove away but I was foiled again as he'd parked out of sight. A lot of clients preferred to park at the end of my road rather than in the driveway. I always told clients that no one in the houses near me knew what I did for a living so they were welcome to park on my drive but many of them didn't want to risk it and I don't blame them. Obviously that particular kind of job where I didn't get to see their faces was risky as I was well aware that they could have whipped out a knife instead of their cock and cut my throat. I was putting my life in danger and I knew it but I felt I could trust them. Looking back I realise how fortunate I am to still be here.

The cheekiest 'visitor' I had booked me for an hour. There isn't anything interesting to tell you about that particular interlude. When we came downstairs afterwards I realised he hadn't given me my fee and mentioned it to him. He smacked his hand off his forehead and said "Shit I've left my wallet in the van, I'll go and get it". Now some of the escort women I knew would have followed him out the door to his van but I didn't. 'He went off out the front door and down the end of the road where, once again his vehicle was out of sight. I expect you know what I'm going to say... yes, I never saw him again. I was annoyed of course but it's all a learning curve in the escorting game. Although Id been doing it a few months at that point, I realised that you just can't trust all of them. Tina who I mentioned earlier told me she went out on an outcall one day and was taken into some woods by her client. They went on to have sex and then when he had got dressed he just ran off never to be seen again! She was furious but got no sympathy from me, I thought it was so funny.

I've tried food sex once in my life and this was with a client. He turned up at my house with4 Magnum ice creams, and where it didn't end up isn't worth mentioning. It was everywhere- he and I were plastered in it, as was the bed and the floor. After he left I had to pay someone to come and clean the carpet. It wouldn't have been so bad if they'd been white chocolate ones. He did ring me again asking if he could make another appointment to see me and I said yes as long as you don't bring any food-he didn't get in touch again, and I was glad. I also removed 'food sex' from the 'things I like' list on my profile!

On one occasion, a middle aged guy turned up on my doorstep with a carrier bag in his hand. He hadn't mentioned that he wanted anything out of the norm when he booked the appointment to see me (mind you, what is norm in this line of work, I suppose.) I asked him what was in his bag and he said, "Something you will enjoy". I took him at face value, he looked respectable enough and with some trepidation, off we went, up into the boudoir. He opened his carrier bag and pulled out 2 rolls of black pvc. tape, about 4inches wide.

'And what do you think you're going to do with that'? I asked him- if he'd have suggested bondage, I'd have thrown him straight out) He told me he wanted to wrap my boobs up in it....?! It sounded harmless enough so I told him he could. He told me to sit on the edge of the bed while he got to work-Well basically let's just say there was just too much of me and too little tape.... He'd have needed at least 10 rolls of it to go round my ample bosom. As he was trying to stretch it round my naked boobs he said "I don't think we're going to have enough" (no shit Sherlock, I thought) By the time he'd finished I looked like I'd been wrapped in overstretched bin liners.... the tape was flapping everywhere and it just wasn't the desired effect he had hoped for. He stepped back to admire his handiwork and commented "you're bigger than I thought you would be". I thought, 'well pardon me all over the place!!' He then took me from behind, rougher than was necessary, possibly to work off his frustrations and then left. I never saw him again!

The most surprising client I had was a policeman. He came to see me once a fortnight. After our first meeting he pulled out his badge and showed it to me with an unreadable look on his face... I said, 'Oh shit, you're not going to arrest me are you? Is that a real badge? ''yes it is' he replied, and he then went on to tell me not to panic, I wasn't in any kind of trouble and he was only there for the sex! I did ask him if what I was doing was illegal and he said that escort work is obviously a grey area in the eyes of the law. The ladies standing on street corners, as we all know, are often arrested but the independent escorts, like myself working from home were ok. Entertaining men in the privacy of your own home is acceptable... and if there was a problem and questions asked- it would be very difficult for anyone to prove that money was paid to a woman for sexual services. He did make a comment about the taxman liking to get his hands on me and I wondered if that was a double entendre?!

A client I was very fond of, was the double of Pavarotti. Not what I'd consider an attractive body but he had a very gentle voice and in bed he almost had me singing opera! He had the most amazing tongue and gave me multiple orgasms. The down side was that he had the smallest penis I have ever encountered... it resembled a button and that's being generous. Having said that, be assured that when my phone rang and his number flashed up, I smiled with anticipation of seeing him. I did bump into him in the supermarket once. He was in the fresh fruit section with a woman who I assumed to be his wife. They were holding a grapefruit each and when he glanced across and saw me he nearly dropped the grapefruit on his foot. I winked at him and carried on with my shopping.

One young guy called Simon used to visit me regularly. He was about 5ft 11 inches tall, crew cut hairstyle and clean shaven. A stocky muscular build and a hairy chest to die for-I fancied him rotten. During his first visit to me he said "can I ask you something?" I thought "here we go".... He went on to say that he didn't want sex with me, he just wanted to cuddle up and talk to me for the hour he had booked to see me. I thought what a lovely simple request that was. He liked me to stroke his hair and we would lay there chatting about life in general and that was it. He was so hunky but so sweet. I admit that after seeing him about 4 times I did ask him if there was any chance that we could have sex one day. He said "No because it will spoil things" That was the first rejection Id had in a very long time, and I confess to feeling very disappointed! Every time he left me I was as horny as Hell and was always glad when I had another client after Simon had gone!

One day, a guy in his forties came to see me. As pre-arranged on the phone, I was upstairs waiting for him. He let himself in, picked up a pair of my black silk stockings that he'd requested I leave on the telephone table for him in the hall downstairs. He went into the downstairs loo, popped the stockings on, removed all other clothing, and I listened as he came upstairs. As you can imagine, appointments like these made me feel nervous and excited. I didn't know who would be coming through the door. This man appeared in my bedroom doorway and as I noted how attractive he was despite the stockings which looked ridiculous-.he said,

"Oh my God, I feel fantastic, this is great!"

'It's nice to meet you too' I laughed 'why don't you come and join me over here?' We proceeded to have a mutually satisfying hour together and I admit I did like the feel of the stockings on him... until, after business was over, he asked me to peel the stockings off. I obliged but snagged one of them on my fingernail... I was inwardly fuming as they'd cost a bloody fortune!

CHAPTER 21

Another episode I recall was being on my hands and knees In my sexy attire on the kitchen floor waiting for my first meeting with a new client... it wasn't actually a meeting as all he wanted to do was let himself in the house, find me in the kitchen and take me doggy style on the floor without a word being spoken-.before he entered me I reached round to check he was wearing a condom, and I would like to mention here that I did go for 6monthly sexual health check-ups. One of the questions the nurses ask you when you first go to the clinic is 'Why do u feel you need to make an appointment for a sexual health check-up?' Down to earth as ever I replied, 'Because I do escort work' The nurses laughed at this and wanted to hear about some of my exploits, I used to look forward to my appointments as it was quite a giggle. Another bonus was that they always packed me off with lots of free condoms! Anyway, back to this client-we never got to see each other's faces. As I'm writing all these incidents down I realise what a risky life I was leading but at that time it was all such a thrill and that's the truth of it. Lots of sex, lots of money and a feeling of being in total control of what I was doing.

CHAPTER 22

To my surprise one day, I had a call from a lady! It crossed my mind that it could be from an angry wife/ girlfriend who had discovered her other half had been coming to see me. I held the phone away from my ear, bracing myself for a screaming voice in the earpiece... This wasn't the case. This lady asked me if her and her husband could come and see me for an hour as she wanted to give her hubby their first threesome for his birthday. I agreed but only after telling her that she and he must really talk about this idea properly and be sure they both wanted to do it. She said they would and in anticipation of their date with me, I went on a website and bought a big red body bow.

On the big day, and with a lot of foul language, I managed to wrap the bow around myself (I made a better job of it than the twit with the Pvc tape) I put some stockings on, thigh length boots and waited for them to arrive. When they turned up he looked more nervous than his wife (and do bear in mind that this was not only their first threesome, it was also her first experience of being intimate with another woman.) I didn't often offer my clients alcohol but I felt a cup of tea just wasn't going to cut it (and it was his birthday after all) so I gave them both a glass of red wine and we sat for 10 minutes in the lounge chatting, with me trying to relax them a bit. I did notice that hubby looked like he had a pair of socks down the front of his undies and thought that it was a good sign... Anyway up we go to the bedroom and I must admit I felt nervous too. There's one thing taking part in group sex at the swingers club but being with alone with a married couple was a whole new ballgame. They were a clean nice looking couple in their late 30s. She was a petite brunette and he was over 6ft tall with receding brown hair. After undressing each other at my request (oh all that power!!) a bit of giggling and shuffling about the 3 of us laid on my bed with her in the middle. Now I've always been quite happy being a big lady-, it has never bothered me.-.but I felt like a giant next to her and I told her so. She laughed and said "don't worry about it, he's always fantasising about big women". We'd been laying on the bed for about five minutes giggling and fumbling about. I asked them both if I could remover her pants and she seemed happy with that idea whereas he kind of croaked out a "yes". Off they came, and after playing with her boobs while he watched, I moved my hand down to open her legs. I was all set to fondle her, we'd been having a nice kiss and cuddle and I felt she was ready to go further. Maybe I shouldn't disappoint you all and spin you an erotic tale of what happened next but this is an honest story and I don't want to tell porkies. All of a sudden, hubby leaps off the bed and ran out the door and into the bathroom, slamming the door behind him, shouting "I can't do this I'm sorry". She and I just looked at each other in silence for a moment and she then said she was, in her own words, "fucking livid" She explained they'd been discussing and plucking up the courage to see me for weeks and had convinced each other they were ready to give it a go. She apologised for wasting my time and insisted I keep the money they'd given me (I had intended to give it back) She said she would have liked things to have gone further with her and I, as she had been enjoying it. She then went and hooked hubby out the bathroom and he emerged red faced with embarrassment and mumbling apologies. They left my house and I never heard from either of them again. I hope they patched things up and that no major problems arose after the event. And after all that, my big red bow was still in position and I was disappointed not to have been unwrapped!

CHAPTER 23

There was only one time during my time doing the escort work that I was left feeling guilty and ashamed of what I was doing after a client left me. A guy probably in his 30s came to see me for an hour appointment. Everything was going well and straightforward, when after about twenty five minutes his mobile suddenly rang. He rummaged around in his trouser pocket to find it and when he answered it he said nothing for a couple of minutes apart from "Ok, I'm on my way" I asked him if everything was alright and he replied "my misses has just gone into labour-Hang on, let me give you some money" I sat there and was suddenly hit by a huge feeling of guilt. I watched him quickly trying to get back in his clothes and thought was an asshole he was visiting me when his wife was due to have their child. I said

"Forget the money, I don't want it, use it to buy your wife some flowers". He replied "oh cheers love" and off he went. It was one of the rare occasions I really sat and thought about what I was doing, I did feel sorry for the wives/girlfriends of the men I saw, but not sorry enough to give up the job I have to admit. If I'm honest, I was hooked on hooking and wouldn't have given up unless I really had to. If nothing else positive came from that meeting, I realised I still had a conscience which made me realise that although I was living this unconventional life, I hadn't turned into a hard faced whore-a whore, yes but I hadn't lost my compassionate nature and it was a relief to realise that.

I stated on my profile that I was happy to see disabled guys as long as the disability wasn't too severe. One of my favourite clients was a man in his sixties who had bowel cancer. I did feel so sorry for him, he was such a sweet man. He did tell me before our first appointment that he had a bag attached to his tummy which his bodily waste went into and asked if he could come round so I could see it, then if it put me off, he would go on his way with no offence taken. He assured me that it didn't smell so I agreed to see him.

His needs were very simple, he liked me to get on top of him, just straight sex. I just did my best to forget about his "bag", which rested to the side of his belly button and got on with it, I did enjoy seeing the pleasure he got from me. He told me that all the other women he'd tried to book appointments with, refused to see him because of his bag, which I thought was sad but at the same time I could understand it.

Another disabled guy I used to see had Parkinson's disease. He told me the same as the chap with cancer had, that many escorts refused to see him. He sounded nice enough on the phone and I told him when I would be able to see him. When he arrived Id estimate him to be in his 40s, very slim and attractive. He was shaking a little but I thought that might be nerves! He sat on the edge of my bed and started undressing himself-I offered to help him but he refused to let me, though he did ask me to help him take off his shoes and socks (all in a day's work!) He was still shaking a little-. Possibly nerves as well as the Parkinson's perhaps?! I asked him what position would be most comfortable for him and he asked that I climb on top of him. After some foreplay he said "I'm ready now" and I hopped on. I was going up and down for what seemed like ages and after awhile.my thighs were killing me, it had never taken this long before, and I started thinking I was losing my touch so I asked him if he was ok.

'I came ages ago but didn't like to say as you seemed to be enjoying yourself!" he replied. Obviously with his trembling and shaking because of the Parkinson's as well as the condom he was wearing, I didn't realise he had already cum. Afterwards he let me help him get dressed and off he went. I did see him a couple more times after that, bless him.

CHAPTER 24

I had several clients who didn't drive and occasionally I would pick them up from my local train station, or I'd pick them up as they got off the bus. The only problem with doing this was that I had to cover my naughty clothes with more conservative daywear. Then, when we arrived at my house I'd just whip the outer layers off revealing what I had on underneath. I felt it kind of spoiled the moment really -it's so much better when a client turned up on the doorstep and saw me standing there with next to nothing on, much more sexy (such brave men!!) One man I had picked up from the train station was so excited to see me that we didn't even get to my house! En route, he ran his hand up the outside of the trousers I was wearing.

'Oh my God, you've got stockings on under there' he exclaimed,

'Of course I have, you like them then?' I replied, smiling,

'I've got a boner now, can we stop somewhere?'

'My house is 10 minutes away, it would be better to be comfortable' I told him. He begged me to find a secluded spot, which is very easy in Darkest Deepest Dorset-there are more fields than you can shake a stick at-so I found a lane and parked at the end of it. He leapt over the front seats into the back and couldn't get his trousers down quick enough. I went down on him like an obliging hooker does and it was game over within 3 minutes!

'I've got to wait an hour and a half for my train back' he went on to inform me,

'Can we go back to yours and wait there until you run me back to the station?'

This annoyed me to be honest but I agreed and drove us back to mine, where we sat for over an hour in silence, there was just nothing to talk about really. I made him 2 cups of tea then dropped him back. I was surprised he didn't want a repeat performance at my house but obviously he'd done his bit and that must have been sufficient!

I said earlier that I've been fortunate enough not to have had anything nasty happen to me by anyone during my escort days. I'm sitting here tapping away and I have remembered an incident which did scare the hell out of me. As well as outcalls, Id started doing "car meets". Now this was a dangerous thing to do and I've since asked myself what on earth possessed me to do it? Had I been mad? It's not like I needed the money, let's face it, but some guys didn't want to come to my house and couldn't afford to see me in hotels so the car was the only other option for a meet. When I told my best friend what I was doing she insisted I show her where I went for the car meets and we had an arrangement whereby I would text her when I was off to do one, and then text her when I got back home to let her know I was safe. I met clients in a car park near my home, they would jump in my car and I'd take them to the end of a secluded lane. These were my rules as I felt it was safer to have them in my car with me, as opposed to either me going with them in their car or them following me to the lane in their car. On one occasion I didn't text her quickly enough for her liking and she was frantic with worry. Did I get a telling off when she finally got hold of me!

CHAPTER 25

On one particular occasion I agreed to a car meet with a guy. It was pitch black up the end of this lane and a freezing cold December evening. I kept the interior light on so we could see what we were doing. As I leaned towards him with the intention of kissing him, he leaned back away from me, then went in his trouser pocket and pulled out a pair of long yellow rubber gloves. My heart dropped, my blood just froze in my veins and everything people had warned me would happen to me one day came into my mind. I really believed he was going to strangle me in my car. It's the only time in my life I can say I knew what fear feels like, I was terrified. I managed to say (it came out more like a squeak) "what's that?" whilst grabbing the door handle preparing to jump out the car if necessary- He looked at me very calmly and said

"Rubber gloves"

'Yes I can see that' I replied, what the Hell are they doing in your pocket? He then went on to tell me he suffers from OCD and is paranoid about touching most things so feels more comfortable with the gloves on. Well I nearly collapsed with relief and told him I thought he was going to strangle me to which he just laughed and said "no you're safe with me young lady... you don't mind the gloves do you?!!" After that we did have some foreplay which, as you can imagine, did feel very strange as he kept the gloves on the whole time. I climbed on top of him on the back seat and rode him until he had an orgasm. And that, my dear readers, was the last car meet I ever did. Probably for the best I think. I remember my best friend looking very relieved when I told her there'd be no more of those happening. Having said all that the car meets were fun up to that point, being taken from behind over the bonnet and almost getting caught by a farmer who came along at an unfortunate moment... all good fun but the gloves thing really was a wakeup call to the potential danger I was putting myself in. And I have to add that to this day I've never seen a pair of rubber gloves that go up above the elbow, like his did!

When a client I'd never seen before turned up on the door step, I opened the front door and looking hard at my chest, he said,

"Mm the rolling hills of Dorset!" Smiling at his remark I invited him in. He looked around the hallway and said "I bet you do well here". When I asked him what he meant, he said that I was the only one on the website in my area. He went on to tell me that all the others were in towns a few miles away from the village I lived in. After our half hour together he told me he'd definitely come back to see me (he did) and that he was pleased I was exactly as Id described myself on my profile. Apparently many a randy guy has turned up on a working lady's doorstep and had a shock when he realised she'd told various porkies on her profile and was nothing like she'd described (the women didn't always use photos of themselves, (tut tut) Anyway, his comment led me to be curious about other sex workers around and I decided to check out the competition on the website. As I looked through the hundreds of other women... I was amazed at how many there were... I was amused at some of the profiles as some of them portrayed themselves to offer an upper-class service, and some catered only for business men. Well as far as I'm concerned any man can put a suit and tie on and carry a brief case, not only that, what did these women think they were offering that was so superior and different to the rest of us? We were all in the same line of work and what men want by the end of the appointment is pretty much the same... to have an orgasm! And the prices these women charged, good grief... some wanted £150.00 for half an hour and anything up to £500.00 an hour. Good luck to them though if they were able to earn that type of money but I'll never understand why men would want to pay so much. The most money I ever earned was doing an overnight outcall. I went and met the client in a hotel at 8pm, and left in the morning at 8am. For that I earned a £1000.00. I was asked a few times to do overnighters but I refused as I didn't like leaving my daughter which may surprise you or you might not believe me, but despite the strange life I was leading, I was still a mum and made sure my daughters needs were met to the best of my ability. Many a time I would look at her sweet little face, and feel ashamed at what I was doing but I also had no desire to give it up at that point.

Some of my clients came to me wanting a massage only which surprised me. I was honest and told them I'm not a qualified masseur but would do my best! I'd still dress up in my work clothes just in case they changed their minds but none of them did. I quite enjoyed those appointments as it was nice to be able to relax and chat, and occasionally I'd have the bonus of them giving me a massage-bliss!

Chapter 26

I received an email one day from a guy who said he was also an escort on the same website as me, and he'd read my profile. He asked me if I'd consider teaming up with him to work and felt we could make a "killing". He asked me to check out his profile and let him know what I thought. When I found his profile I nearly died... he reminded me of a ferret and whoever had taken his photos must have had a job keeping a straight face-.I've seen more meat on a butchers pencil! Apparently he was 28 but he looked more like 50 from what I could see. Out of curiosity I looked at what he charged for his services-I burst out laughing when I saw he was charging just £20.00 for half an hour, and £35.00 for an hour! I then went on to look at other guys profiles and noticed that apart from a couple of them on the list, who were attractive and probably were earning ok, the rest were a collection of horror stories, all charging a very small amount for their "services"... I realised, as you probably have, that they weren't worried about escorting, they just wanted some sex! Even if one of the better looking fellas had sent me the same email as the first guy had, asking me to pair up for work Id have refused anyway as I liked to be fully in control of what I was doing. Being independent and not reliant on anyone else suited me perfectly.

A married couple once emailed me asking if I would join them for an evening at their house to play the role of a Dominatrix. Their speciality on the website was Sado /masochism and apparently they were very much in demand. They offered me a very generous fee to join them and told me that all that I would be required to do, would be to wear thigh length boots, a black body stocking (oh my God, with my figure?!) and whip clients who wanted it. I declined their offer as I just couldn't inflict pain on anyone, whether they were enjoying it or not! I was asked by new clients many times, what my speciality was and I used to tell them, 'I don't specialise in anything, I'm just a good all-rounder really!'

I realised that working from the family home wasn't ideal and considered using some of my cash stash to set myself up in a flat somewhere, it would be used strictly for work purposes. I posted a message on the escort website asking if any other ladies would be interested going into this with me. My idea was that if there were 3 or four bedrooms, a couple of ladies could rent a couple of the rooms from me and chip in with bills. I had endless replies from working girls who were keen to do it as some of them were desperate to find somewhere to work from. I was pleased with the response and started looking for somewhere suitable. After a couple of weeks I found the perfect place- a 3 bedroom bungalow in a very discreet location, away from prying eyes and not far from my home. During this time I was meeting a lot of the ladies interested in my proposition-.I had to put the work on hold as I was running about like a headless chicken trying to sort things out, much to some of my clients disappointment. Eventually I chose 2 of the women Id met. I trusted my instincts that they would be ok to be part of my plan and I then met the landlord of the property to discuss rent etc. As far as he was concerned I was a married woman, whose husband worked away, with a child and he seemed happy for "us" to move in, saying he would give me his bank details within a couple of days and give me a moving in date. Myself and my would be "housemates" were very excited and looking forward to setting up shop! The whole plan went tits up when Tina... you remember I mentioned her earlier, told me not forget the whole idea as it was too risky. The main problem she said I might have is that I didn't know the other women well enough to be able to trust them to pay me for their rooms and as she pointed out, they could be drug takers, alcoholics or God knows what else. I was disappointed but realised she was right, It was a real gamble and if they messed up in any way, it could cause me a lot of problems. I was dreading telling the others that the plan was off and made up some cock and bull reason for this latest turn of events. Neither of them were happy about it, neither was I, but I think Tina was right and I'm glad I took her advice. I just continued to work from home, the same as I'd always done.

CHAPTER 27

I got used to strange phone calls. A man rang up one day and told me he wasn't very well off and could he come and see me but pay me less than I charged. My answer to that was along the lines of, I'm sorry about your money problems but my fee is as it is, take it or leave it. He then went on to call me every filthy fucking whore under the sun, and who the hell did I think I was earning more than nuclear physicists? Now I'm not sure if that last bit is true, I doubt it, but I ended the conversation telling him he sounded sexually frustrated and to go and get laid if anyone would have him, as it might do him some good!!

I received a call one day from an American guy. He told me he was in the UK with his 13 year old son and he wanted to bring his son round to see me so I could take the lads virginity while "Dad" watched. He offered me £1000.00 (he even offered to pay before turning up, using PayPal so the money would go straight into my account). When you're in this line of work you get to a point where nothing surprises you but I went silent with shock at what he'd asked me. I then told him there was no amount of money he could offer me that would persuade me to do what he wanted. I told him I thought he was disgusting and that I'm not into paedophilia and ended the call. The mind boggles doesn't it? During the 2 years I was doing the escort work, I was often asked if I would have sex with various animals to which I replied No. Like most normal people, I find all that kind of thing very offensive and just can't get my head around the fact that some people like to do it.

When I answered my phone one day, a male voice said,

'Can I hoist your tits up?' Just came out with it like that, no hello nothing,

'I beg your pardon?'

'Do you have a pulley thing that hangs from your ceiling so that I can hoist your tits up?'

'I have absolutely no idea what you're talking about but my bedroom has a bed and other furniture in it, the only thing hanging from the ceiling is a light,'

'Shame cos your tits would look great pulled right up'

'I'm sure they would but not in this lifetime, goodbye'. And with that I ended the call. What a complete idiot honestly!!

I saw several clients who would get undressed, lay on the bed with me and then be hit with a guilt attack for what they were doing. These guys would apologise, say they were embarrassed and then go on their way. I did offer to give them their money back and only one fella took it back. The rest said that I could keep it as they had wasted my time. All quite sad really, but the counselling business wasn't my department. I probably sound hard at times, but I had to be to a certain extent. Being an escort is quite a balancing act. I was friendly towards the guys I saw but firm too. If you're not they would take all sorts of advantages and I couldn't allow that.

CHAPTER 28

As you can tell, I was a busy bee during this time. I even had calls, emails and texts asking if I was going to be available on Christmas Day! Probably from guys fed up with the festivities and needing some light relief. I turned my phone off on Christmas Day and when I turned it back on the day after Boxing Day there were several missed calls and texts. I did have to remind some of my clients that I did have a family life as well as a working one! Like any working parent it was all a juggling act. When Andrew came home from work every weekend I would just do cam and phone work from home but occasionally I did sneak off to do the odd car meet! Andrew never complained and still seemed happy with our 'open' relationship. We seemed to be jogging along nicely. I was able to buy lots of nice things for my family and myself with my earnings and generally life was a bit crazy but in my eyes, good. I frequently got asked if I would accompany guys overseas for business trips or just holidays and if I could, I would have accepted. Having my daughter made it very difficult to be able to do that though and I had to turn down the offer of trips to Dubai, South Africa and Mexico. What really cheesed me off one day was reading one of the sex workers blogs about the fantastic 10 days she'd had in Mexico with the client who had asked me but I'd had to turn down... what a bummer. I was often asked by friends how Andrew and I could live like we did, having sex with other people and him allowing me to do the escort work. It was a difficult question to answer really, it just seemed to work for us both at that time.

It used to annoy me that, although you stated clearly the services you wouldn't offer, it didn't stop men asking.-anal was the most common request and I always told them off for asking. Another car meet I recall was with a guy who asked me If I'd mind him filming me and him having sex. I was reluctant and worried that the video would pop up on the internet somewhere. He gave me his word that it would be for his own personal use and against my better judgement, I gave him the go ahead to do it. To my knowledge, up to now anyway, he was true to his word and thankfully my performance hasn't popped up anywhere I wouldn't want it to.

CHAPTER 29

There's a website where men can check out reviews of sex workers in different areas and read opinions of guys who'd used their services. I went on there one day to be nosey, and I was really shocked when I saw my work name on there. I braced myself to read what people were saying about me... it may seem odd to you reading this, but I am sensitive and have my insecurities like a lot of other people. Well, I sure picked the right time for a read.... an almighty online row was in progress, and all about yours truly! I scrolled back to the start of their conversation and some fellas were saying what I was like and I was well worth a visit, I was described by some as big and beautiful, others said I was genuinely nice, not hard faced like some of the other escorts they'd seen, and other generally positive things about me. One guy didn't agree with the others. He said I was "a pig in pants" (I know one of my friends reading this will be howling with laughter at this point!) and he went on to ask how a fat bird can possibly be attractive? He then got personal towards larger people in general and said they all smell. Lots of people, including women got involved in the conversation and the "fat debate" got really heated. I sat there feeling really crushed and upset but felt compelled to read on regardless. I'm glad I did as I got a lot of support from the other guys which cheered me up a bit. To this day, I don' t know who the guy running me down was, because every man Id entertained up to that point had gone away "satisfied" and seemed happy when they left me, so I don't know who he was. I also don't know who the men were, sticking up for me, but if any of you are reading this, "Cheers guys!" And as the saying goes, "You can't please "em all!

CHAPTER 30

As well as the in calls I was doing from my home, there were also the outcalls. I would travel within a reasonable distance and earn nearly double the fee I'd get for in calls. I went to see one old boy who must have been in his 70s (not pleasant I admit, but hey ho, some of them still have their needs) and all he wanted me to do for a whole two hours was bite and suck his nipples and that was it... that's all I had to do. Easy money yes, but oh was I bored and so glad when the time was up! Apparently the wife was in Belgium visiting her sister on that occasion.

Another old gent I used to visit occasionally, was a widower. He had a shed in the garden. All he wanted me to do was go in the shed with him, strip down to my undies then sit on his lap and smoke a cigarette in a cigarette holder, then blow the smoke in his face. No sex, just smoking the cigarette-I did ask him why he enjoyed it so much-he smiled and said "you wouldn't understand." With my older client's, it often crossed my mind that one of them might die on me one day- can you imagine that?? Fortunately it never happened-sorry to disappoint you! Although I was only with this old boy for about 10 minutes, he still paid me for half an hour. When I did outcalls at weekends or during evenings when my daughter was at home, a friend of mine would come over and babysit for me while I went out. I would pay her which helped her out too. I expect many of you are thinking how sordid this all sounds and what an awful Mum I am, doing all these things with a young child and I can understand why you would think like that. I did feel guilty sometimes but escorting became very addictive and I was genuinely enjoying my life. I felt like a business woman, I had my appointment book, a little case that Id pop my toys in for outcalls and I was loving every minute of it. A lot of my friends said they would love to be able to do what I was doing and I'd say to them if you want to earn money easily it's the ideal way to do it, but you need rules you must stick to including taking steps to stay as safe as you can and don't let it take over your life. I also told them it's not for the faint hearted! I admit that it was taking over my life before it all came to an end. I worked nearly every day, and it was tiring but the thrill of it all kept me going. Sometimes I'd do outcalls in Travel lodges (I must have been to every single one in the southwest of England) I regularly frequented hotels and bed and breakfasts. The client would pay for the accommodation and if I was lucky some of them took me out for lunches or dinners, paying for the meals as well as me for my time.

One of my favourite outcalls was with four lovely squaddies! One of them had rung me and asked if I would meet them in a hotel and let all of them have sex with me. I told him I would prefer it if I could bring a friend with me, which he agreed to, and told him to ring me the following day. I rang Tina and asked her if she would come along with me and join in as I was nervous about being on my own with four men. She said she would be happy to help me out and when the guy rang me back, we arranged to meet at a Travelodge about an hour from where I lived. The appointment was to be for an hour and we agreed the guys would pay me £750.00 which I would split with Tina. When we arrived at the Travelodge, the squaddies had booked two rooms, two of them sharing each room. We knocked on the door of the room he had told me they would be in, waiting for us. When he opened the door Tina and I started smiling from ear to ear. He was in his twenties and behind him, his three friends were draped across 2 single beds smiling and waving at us. We went in, headed straight for the bathroom so we could get dressed up for them. We were giggling like a pair of schoolgirls when we were getting ready; in anticipation of what we just knew would be a fantastic hour. And it was. They were all lovely lads, all young, fit and eager to please us two older ladies! I find younger men gentler and better kissers than older guys which is a very good start! We spent the hour giving and receiving oral sex, had lots of foreplay and full sex in many different positions. They didn't ask Tina and I to play with each other which surprised us and we were secretly pleased. We would have done it to please them but neither of us were really wanted to. It was a very noisy hour and I hoped that there wasn't anyone in the rooms either side of us! After the hour was over, one of the guys gave us our fee we got dressed back into our 'normal clothes' and off we went walking as if we had just got off a motorbike after a three hour ride!

I won't ever forget my first ride in a limo. One of my clients called Don, was a private hire driver. He asked me if I'd like to go out with him for a drive in the limo- well how could I possibly refuse. The plan was to find somewhere secluded and have some fun before he had to go on to pick up a party of women for a 50th birthday bash. As we were going along I was quite happy sitting in the back with the disco lights and music on, drink in hand just enjoying the luxury of the lovely slow drive. Suddenly I saw lights flashing behind us and to my horror the police indicating that we should pull over. Don obliged, (he was swearing a lot) then the policeman knocked on his window. I was trying to cover myself up unsuccessfully as I was wearing some sexy undies and little else. The reason we'd been stopped? Because he said Don was driving too slowly!! That's the first time I'd heard of that happening. When the officer asked Don why he was driving so slow, he replied that it was because I had never been in a limo before and that he was treating me because I'd been going through a rough patch. Anyway, the policeman told us to speed up a bit and sent us on our way. This little incident put a damper on the evening and when we did find somewhere we thought would be ideal to have sex, Don drove too fast into a field and hit some bumps. We parked up, had our romp then he drove me back to the place Id left my car. I didn't hear any more from him until the next day when he rang and told me that after dropping me off, he was a couple of miles up the road and got a puncture (due to the earlier bumps I supposed) He ended up being late picking up the birthday party ladies. They complained to his boss who then gave him a severe telling off- Not only for being late but because one of the partygoers found a dildo under one of the cushions on the back seat.... oops. I never heard from him after that which was no surprise and I was always left wondering what happened to the dildo as I never did get it back!

I'd arranged to meet one guy at a Travelodge for an hour's appointment and he sounded really nice on the phone. He told me he would be standing in the car park, and what he would be wearing. Well I've spun into the car park, and saw this man in a long black coat and I'm not exaggerating when I tell you, he was an absolute ringer for Max Wall-some of you might remember him on the television years ago. A revolting looking man with a bald head on top, but hair hanging down around the sides which covered his ears. He watched me drive in and waved at me frantically... I looked at him, drove right around him and out the car park.... I just couldn't have got intimate with him, he looked truly horrible. I looked in my rear view mirror and he was shouting at me to come back and still waving.... "Wave on" I thought and couldn't get out of the car park quick enough! I just could not have got intimate with him, he was horrible!

CHAPTER 31

One of my regular guys called Clive rang me one winters evening. He wanted an hour booking with me but said he wanted to do something different and have sex outside somewhere. 'Where did you have in mind?' I asked him, 'We can go where I do the car meets, its private there.'

No' he replied, 'I've been scouting around and found the ideal place. I'll come to your house and you follow me in your car' If I hadn't met him before I would have refused but he was ok and I trusted him, so I agreed to go. My friend was happy to come round and babysit for an hour, he turned up soon afterwards and off we went. I'd been following him for only 10 minutes when he turned into an area on the outskirts of the village which was known as a beauty spot because of the stunning views. It was really cold this particular night in early December and he said, 'It's bloody freezing, let's just do it in the car' which I thought was a much better idea. I was wearing a long skirt and no knickers with a blouse and cardigan-trying to combine naughty with practical for the weather conditions! We were in the car on the back seat having a kiss, cuddle and a grope-the windows were steaming up nicely and all of a sudden I heard a car approaching and headlights shining on our windscreen. I went to sit up but

Clive pushed me back down and told me to ignore it. I felt a bit uneasy as it was pitch black and I didn't like the thought that another car was in close proximity. Then I heard another engine. And another. This time I insisted on looking out to see what was going on. Now I had often been asked if I liked dogging and I would tell people I had never tried it as it didn't appeal to me. Well that was all about to change. I turned to Clive and said,

'This is a dogging site isn't it?' He confessed that yes it was and he thought if he told me I wouldn't have agreed to go with him. I told him off but then I thought to myself it would be another experience to try. And I have to say that apart from the freezing weather I had a great time. People were jumping in and out of each other's cars, playing with each other, and having full sex while others watched through the car windows. It was like an outdoor version of swingers really. Clive and I were on my backseat with me on top of him, he told me we should leave the headlights on so that other doggers could see that we were happy with anyone to come and watch. A guy stuck his head in through the window and asked if he could jump in with us which we said he could and he sat in the front seat but turned round so he could watch us while he wanked himself off. I found it all an erotic experience, but it really was cold which spoiled it a bit for me. I was amazed to see women bent over the bonnets of cars, knickers down by their ankles, being taken from behind by guys. Some of these women were dressed to please and if they were cold, they didn't let it spoil their fun! Apparently, according to Clive these dogging sessions were a twice weekly event in that area which I had known nothing about. Just goes to show that there's more to village life than a cream tea! Just makes me wonder how it went on regularly like that without anyone stumbling across it all and ringing the police-but then again, the risk of getting caught is part of the thrill. I only went there that one time and although I enjoyed it, I preferred the warmth of the swingers club!!

CHAPTER 32

I had a nice little arrangement with Felicity, the owner of the swingers club. She would let me see clients in one of her caravans during Amy's school holidays, and I'd give her a small amount for the use of it. I also got a lot of my clients into the swinging scene as one of the services I started offering was to accompany guys to the club-Felicity did well out of my nefarious goings on, as I was bringing her extra business. One day, one of my regular clients plucked up the courage to come with me to the club and after a long while persuading him to join myself and a few others in the Jacuzzi, he stripped off and got in. I undressed quickly, keen to get in because despite my line of work and the swinging, I was usually covered up if only a little and was still quite shy about being seen completely naked. Anyway, as I went in after him I slipped. You already know I'm a big lady... I'm not joking when I tell you, I landed like an elephant in the water and swear I must have emptied most of it. As I tried to save myself I noticed 3 very worried looking men with their hands held out in front of them ready to grab them... sorry, me....!" Bloody hell Abigail" said one of them, "my whole life just flashed before my eyes" It was funny, very embarrassing and no surprise that I never saw that particular client again-think it was all too much for him I think, poor chap:)

Another client who I took to the club was a middle aged Scots man. He was very nervous about his 1st visit to a swingers club and took a bottle of whisky with him, the best part of which he drank while we were there. The booze must have been a great help because he stayed there long after I'd gone and the last I saw of him, he was lying flat on his back in the playroom receiving a blow job from one woman and playing with the other two who were standing either side of the bed. I think it's safe to say he enjoyed himself as he went a few more times after that and without needing me to hold his hand

CHAPTER 33

Prior to starting escort work I'd gone into the red on my bank account. I'd been getting letters from the bank manager threatening to close my account down unless I came to some arrangement with them. While I was working, all the money I was earning was in my house, stuffed in bags, pots, and generally all over the house-I was so busy I rarely had a chance to go into town and put the money in my bank, that's how mad my life had become. One day I decided to pay the bank a visit and the lady manager ushered me into her office. I told her I was there to sort my account out and was in a position to do so as I now had a regular income. Casually, while looking at my account on her computer, she asked me what work I was doing. I shouldn't have said it but I do love to shock and the Devil in me popped up... I said "I'm doing escort work" Well, three things happened at once. She twisted her head round to face me so quickly, I swear she must have cricked her neck. Her eyebrows disappeared up under her fringe causing her glasses to fall down to the tip of her nose. She said in her very posh voice, "are you having me on?" I looked at her and replied "no it's true, I really am and I'm earning a fortune" There was complete silence for about 5 seconds, I noticed a little smile forming on her lips, then we both burst out laughing. She rang the bell on her desk and a member of staff put her head round the door. The manageress said to her, "we might be awhile here, would you bring us both a coffee?" Well, what a chat we had. She asked me a lot of questions about my job and laughed repeatedly. She concluded the conversation by saying "good luck to you, I wish I had your nerve, you've made my day!" And obviously very happy that I'd put my account back in proper order!

CHAPTER 34

I'd been doing the escort work for just over 2 years when a series of events occurred which would change the whole direction of my life. A man called Robert rang me one morning saying he would like to come and see me the same afternoon so I told him where I lived and we arranged a time. Near the time he was due to arrive, he rang me saying he was completely lost and could I give him directions. It occurred to me that it was the 1st time I'd been asked that, and I told him how to find me. When I opened the front door I had no idea, obviously, that this man would become husband number 3. I expect the film "pretty woman" has just crossed your minds but I'm no Julia Roberts and he certainly isn't Richard Gere! He was however drop dead gorgeous (in my eyes anyway) and I couldn't wait to get him up to my bedroom and see his clothes on the floor-which was quite unusual when you consider I'd been getting more than my fair share of sex during the last 2 years. He was a fabulous lover, gorgeous body and we had a nice cuddle at the end of the hour. He did ask me at some point if I should be paying him, instead of the other way round! As we went back downstairs, I suddenly realised I didn't want him to rush off and offered to make him a cup of tea. He stayed for 2 hours chatting with me. I really enjoyed his company and I suppose you'd say we just "clicked". When he left he said he would do his best to see me the following week, but couldn't promise as it depended on what his wife was doing. He did manage to come back to see me soon after that, 'and don't ask me why, or what happened, but I felt really awkward taking his money. We kept in touch with each other by with texts and calls and at some point he arranged another meet with me. When he arrived, I let him in and to my amazement, heard myself saying' I don't want your money anymore'. He looked at me in confusion, no doubt thinking I didn't want to see him again for whatever reason, and I said "No, I didn't mean it like that'. I rang another client I'd arranged to see later in the day and cancelled him (another 1st for me) Robert and I spent a lovely afternoon together and before he head home I told him that when we saw each other again, it wasn't for the money, it was just because I liked him. He looked delighted and said he felt the same about me. He told me he had been married for 12 years but the marriage had broken down during the last few months. He said he couldn't remember the last time he and his wife had made love, and after a while he made the decision to visit an escort just to, as he put it, 'get his rocks off'. On the days I didn't see him, I continued seeing clients as normal but I started to realise I was lacking the enthusiasm for the job that I'd once had, and thought about Robert constantly. I was confused about my feelings, and I couldn't believe Id fallen for someone (totally unprofessional!) but I wasn't prepared to give up my job completely just yet...

CHAPTER 35

Robert and I had been having our affair for about a month-I say affair because although Andrew and I had an open relationship, I think I knew that Robert and I had something special going for us and I never mentioned him to Andrew. Andrew unknowingly pushed Robert and me together when he did something unforgivable which would lead my life in a new direction again. My oldest daughter Lisa was 17 at this time and would come to our house most weekends to stay. At about 3am one Saturday morning, when she was at our house, I was woken by a text on my phone. To my surprise it was from Lisa, It said, 'Mum are you awake, I need to talk to you about something'

'What's up love'? I replied,

'Can we go down to the kitchen?'

'Course we can, see you in a minute 'Well obviously I was intrigued and it seemed odd to be texting each other when she was only in Amy's bedroom at the end of the landing. I met her in the kitchen, she was sitting at the table looking very pale and nervous.

'Oh my God Lisa what's the matter?' I sat down with her and put my arm round her shoulders. With that she burst into tears and explained that just an hour and a half before, she had been asleep, but woke up because she had the feeling someone was in the bedroom with her. When she opened her eyes, she saw Andrew standing right next to the bunk beds, stark naked and just staring down at her as she laid in the bottom bunk. She told me that when he realised she had seen him he turned around and quickly walked out the bedroom. She was so shocked that she grabbed her mobile phone and was just texting her best friend to tell her what had happened when she glanced up and could see Andrew standing on the landing looking at her through the crack in the open door. Once again they made eye contact and this time, she heard him walk along the landing back to our bedroom and shut the door behind. Well, I can tell you, I was absolutely mortified and couldn't believe Andrew, Amy's father could behave in that way. I told Lisa to go back to bed, to try not to be scared and I promised her I would deal with it first thing in the morning. We both went back up to our bedrooms, and shut the doors behind us. I went to Andrew's side of the bed and looked at him sleeping peacefully. And I had an almost overwhelming urge to punch him repeatedly in the face, I was filled with such a rage. Instead I took a spare duvet from the wardrobe and went downstairs to sleep on the sofa. I woke the following morning-after a restless night-and went up to our bedroom. I shook him on the shoulder and said 'Wake up, I want to talk to you'. He came to, looked at me and asked what was wrong.

'I want to know what the Hell you were doing in the girls' room in the middle of the night, stark naked and staring at Lisa.' To my amazement he didn't even try to deny it or, as I had anticipated, say that he must have been sleep walking. He simply looked at me with fear in his eyes and said 'I didn't touch her, I just like to look at her.' I just crumpled on to the edge of the bed. I asked him what was wrong with him and reminded him that we had an open relationship, with free rein to do what we wanted with whomever we wanted. I said that I felt we had an ideal set up and could not believe he could do that to my own daughter. Then something occurred to me which almost took the wind out of me. I remembered a time, about two years prior, when I wanted to use the printer one weekday while he was away at work. When I switched the printer on, about ten sheets of paper came spewing out which must have been in the printing queue. I picked up these pieces of paper and on each sheet, were pornographic pictures of young teenage girls engaged in sex acts with much older men. I remember that I felt shocked at the time as I realised he had obviously tried to print these images to take away in his lorry while he was away-being blunt, to use as wanking material I guessed. At the time, as shocked as I was, I chose not to confront him about it when he came home that weekend, I'm ashamed to admit, because I just wanted to keep the peace. Now looking at him in our bed I realised that he obviously liked young girls.

'You do realise you have just wrecked our relationship don't you?'

'But I didn't touch her Abby, I was only looking at her'

'That's not the bloody point is it? The fact is, we have Amy. What happens when she's older and wants friends to stay for sleepovers, you going to be perving at them as well?' Jesus Christ Andrew, and what if she tells her Dad eh? He'll be over here wanting to kill you and who could blame him? I feel like killing you myself'

He just laid there looking at me and didn't say anything. I told him he better get up, and go out somewhere for the day and not come back until I told him he could. Still silent, he did as I asked and within twenty minutes I heard him go out and slam the front door behind him. I sat down on my bed, head in my hands and decided when he returned later in the day that I was going to throw him out straightaway-I didn't want him to spend another night under my roof. I went into the girls' room and told Lisa what I was going to do. Poor kid, I felt so sorry for her and just kept apologising to her for what he had done. She told me she was terrified when she saw him standing there like that, because she didn't know if he was going to do something awful to her. I asked her if she was going to tell her Dad but she said that she knew if she did, it would cause a lot of problems that might affect Amy. We both talked about the fact that social workers might become involved which would be opening a whole can of worms. She was so upset but very brave and I hugged her, thanking her for being prepared to keep it all quiet. I drove her home later that day and said that she must tell me if she felt she wasn't coping with what had happened and that I would take her for counselling if she ever felt she needed to talk to someone about it-that sounded lame even to my own ears but I would have done anything to help her deal with it if necessary. That evening, I text Andrew and told him to come home and pick up his stuff that I had packed for him. When he came in the house I looked at him and said 'you bloody stupid, stupid man' He said nothing, not even asking if and when he could see Amy again, he just picked up his belongings and left. I sat in the lounge afterwards and cried nonstop for half an hour. I felt devastated and in shock that my life had changed so drastically in 24 hours. Amy wanted to know where her Daddy had gone and that was even more upsetting. I hope she never finds out what he did, whatever age she is and I will always carry that worry that she might. All I can do is cross that bridge when I come to it. I want to make it clear to you that even if I hadn't met Robert when this happened, I would still have kicked Andrew out. How could I possibly let him continue to live with me after what he had done? Lisa would never have wanted to come and visit me again after that and it would have caused all sorts of difficulties. Andrew just had to go and that was it. One of the hardest things about the whole sorry episode is that I got on really well with his family. His mum rang me about a fortnight after I had thrown him out,

'Abigail, I am sorry you and Andrew have parted company, very sad for Amy especially'

'Yes I know that but sometimes these things happen Laura' I wondered what Andrew had told her about us splitting up. She went on,

'I was surprised that it was over something so trivial to be honest' It was then I realised that no, he obviously hadn't told her the truth,

'What did he tell you the reason was Laura?' I asked her,

'Oh, just that you insisted he stay up late on Sunday nights to watch films with you, when he wants to go to bed as he has to get up early for work the next day. He said its making him very tired and that you have been arguing about it'

Well, I didn't expect him to have told her the truth but honestly- surely he could have thought up something better than that?! Now if I was a bitch, I could have told her the truth and then they would know us splitting up wasn't my fault but I didn't think she and his Dad deserved to be hurt like that so I left it. I do miss them and my ex sister in law as they are a lovely family and I did enjoy being part of it when Andrew and I were together,

CHAPTER 36

Obviously with Andrew gone, Robert was coming round to see me much more often and I'm sure that he was pleased about Andrew's departure as it had made it easier for him to spend more time with me. He told me his marriage was on the rocks long before he met me, and he was thinking about leaving his wife, then he wanted him and me to be together. He was always telling me how much he loved me and was so affectionate towards me and I loved it. He bought me a beautiful diamond ring and other gifts and cards. I wasn't used to being treated like that and it just felt so nice. Part of me was still wanting to hang onto my independence and because it hadn't been long since my Andrew had left, I felt it was far too soon to get too involved with anyone else, though I really cared for him and loved it when he was around me. I'd been so used to living my life the way I wanted to that the thought of commitment was quite suffocating. I did continue to see clients, but nowhere near as many as before. Anyway we carried on as we were for a while until one day he said things had come to a head at home and he wanted to move out. I asked him how he felt about finding a place near me then we could continue seeing each other and see how things went and take it from there.

After looking at various possible places to rent, he found one he liked which was 10minutes drive from where I lived. He gave the landlady a deposit and was all set to move in within a few days. On "moving day" I told him I would meet him at his new place and help him move his stuff in. Upon arriving at what was meant to be his new home, I laughed when I saw his car was jam packed full of his belongings and commented I was surprised he got there in one piece as it was hard to see through the windows there was so much stuff.

The landlady came out the house at met us at her gate. She had her apron on and arms folded looking a bit worried. She went on to tell us that Robert wouldn't be able to move in after all because her husband wasn't happy with her taking a male lodger. She said she tried to ring us the day before to tell us, and again that morning but couldn't get a reply. Robert looked at his mobile and pointed out there were no missed calls and told her to give him his deposit back which she did. We were furious. We don't know to this day if her reason for not letting Robert move in was true, but we just couldn't believe she could do that and of course, the next thing we had to think about was what the Hell he was going to do now? He could hardly return to his home as his wife wouldn't have wanted him there after he'd only left that morning (who could blame her?!). I could see he looked worried sick and I felt so sorry for him, I found myself saying "do you want to move in with me till you find somewhere else?" He looked at me with puppy eyes and asked if it would be ok to which I replied, "We haven't got much choice have we?" He moved in, I removed my profile from the escort website and a new chapter in my life had begun. I can't say I put my work clothes in the loft because Robert liked me to wear them for him! After removing my profile I received loads of emails from disgruntled clients asking where I'd gone and what I was doing, where had my profile gone and asking me to keep my phone number so I could still be reached. They were out of luck as Robert told me to cut my work sim card in half which I was happy to do. I had to cut off altogether or I couldn't have moved on. We were very happy living together and all my children met him and thought he was great fun. Robert was a great support to me when my mum was in the last stages of her life, as well as after she passed away and for that I am grateful.

CHAPTER 37

My oldest lad has been in and out of prison since the age of 16 and progressed from being an alcoholic to taking cannabis, and then onto using heroin and becoming addicted. Every time he went to prison, I was always there to try to support him when he came out but it was all in vain. He has been in prison so many times, that he has become institutionalised. He just cannot cope with normal day to day life outside the prison walls. Sadly my other children have seen the worse side of him but they still love him. I feel I've done as much as I can to help him and live in hope that one day he will change-but to do that he has to really want to make those changes. I often wonder if his father's suicide contributed to the way he has turned out, I just don't know. Robert tried so hard to get my lad clean when he came out of prison and move in with us and to try to keep him out of trouble but to no avail I'm sorry to say, and at the time of writing this, my son is serving yet another lengthy prison sentence. Most of his offences are for shop lifting-.he would then sell what he'd stolen and have enough money for his next fix. When he comes out of prison next year I hope he will come and join me in Spain and I will give it one last go to get him on the straight and narrow. I'm not optimistic that he will change but I have decided I have to try one last time.

CHAPTER 38

Three months before the death of my Mum, Robert and I went on holiday to Egypt and had a fantastic time. During a day trip to the Pyramids, he dropped to one knee and asked me to marry him-I was so happy and accepted immediately. My Mum thought the world of him and was delighted when we told her the news. She said that she could at least die with the knowledge that I at last had a good man who would take care of me and she was so happy about that. I felt ready to commit to someone again and really believed he and I would grow old together. We married two months after my mums death and when I discovered she had left me a good sum of money, we decided to emigrate to Spain with Amy. Ben and Lisa live in the UK and are getting on with their own lives and I am in regular contact with them and return to the UK regularly to visit them and my friends. Liam, of course is still in prison serving his sentence.

CHAPTER 39

I came to realise, after moving out here that I married Robert far too quickly, and didn't know him well enough before tying the knot. When I gave up the escort work I felt the time was right to leave that all behind me and I was excited to move onto a new chapter in my life with him. Sadly, one year down the line, I feel bitter and disillusioned as he changed so much when we moved here. He became very moody and had an abrupt harsh mannerism which as a bubbly person, I found very hard to cope with. Every day I would ask him, 'are you ok? You're very quiet' I was constantly thinking I had done something to upset him, even though I knew I hadn't. He was so loving and attentive when we were living in England but all that changed after the move to Spain.

It occurred to me one day that his quietness might be due to him being bored so I asked him if there was any hobby he might like to try. He said he would like a telescope. I went onto the internet and found one in the UK which cost a thousand pounds and bought it for him. I paid a lot on top to have it delivered here and he did perk up and seemed excited while waiting for its arrival. When it eventually came, he put it together, looked into it a couple of times and decided that it was 'a load of crap' After that the telescope sat on the terrace untouched and

I have recently sold it on EBay. I asked him on many occasion if he might be suffering from depression and offered to go and see a doctor with him if he wanted to go but he refused. If I suggested we go anywhere for a day out he refused and seemed to have no interest in anything. Things came to a head a few weeks ago as my 50th birthday approached. His son and daughter in law were over here to visit us and I had booked (and paid for) the 4 of us to go for a meal and a flamenco show for the evening of my birthday. During the same day, I drove the four of us up to Mijas and mentioned to Robert that I would like the four of us to go on a pony and cart ride. He started shouting and swearing, saying he wasn't going on any fucking horse and cart and what a waste of money it all was. I couldn't believe it. I had used the inheritance from my mother to move us over here, he could have whatever he wanted and yet he begrudged me 15euros on a 15 minute horse ride around Mijas. I was furious and not even worried about his family sitting in the back seat, screamed at him that he was the most selfish man I had ever met. The argument continued up into the underground car park and then I wandered off on my own for a walk and to try and calm down. I walked into the little church in the village, lit a candle for my mum, sat on a pew and balled my eyes out. It was a real low point for me and I couldn't believe he could treat me like that. After all that, I decided we might as well forget the night out me had planned as I just can't put a smile on my face and pretend everything's cherry when it obviously isn't. Obviously my 50th birthday was completely ruined and I would never have forgiven him for that as it's a milestone occasion and I think things like that are very important.

CHAPTER 40

As well as that episode, soon afterwards it was our first wedding anniversary. Now after the birthday debacle I thought this would be a chance for him to redeem himself. I told him I was going to meet a friend in town for a coffee and he said he would come to, so that he could buy me an anniversary present. I sat down with my friend and off he went, disappearing among the shoppers. He returned to where we were sitting ten minutes later holding a little bag in his hand.

'I've bought you something really special babe' he informed me. He then went on to say that it was a ring and had cost him 800 euros (he wasn't big on surprises)…. when I asked if I could see it, he said

'no you have to wait till our anniversary' On the big day he gave me my 'present' It was indeed a beautiful eternity ring, 18 carat gold with a setting of seven diamonds. I thanked him and was delighted with it. That evening, I went on my internet banking and to my horror, discovered he had paid for it with my money!! Which led to another screaming match. These are only a few of my moans about Robert, there are many more but his moodiness and selfishness were the main factors to us calling it a day and I ended up throwing him out. The icing on an already deflated cake was when, after throwing him out, he told me he wanted his paperwork, driving license etcetera. While I was gathering it all together, I noticed something wedged in between his debit card and the little plastic sleeve it was in. It was a passport size photo of his ex-wife. He denied point blank putting it in there, trying to convince me that it had probably been in his wallet for ages, but as I pointed out, he only received the debit card recently from the Spanish bank so he must have put her photo in there. That really did hurt me but also made me realise I had done the right thing by ending the relationship. I don't think I will ever understand why Robert changed so much when we moved down here but he had been a psychiatric nurse in a well known hospital for the criminally insane in the UK and I often wondered if the 32 years he worked there, before taking the early retirement had rubbed off on him and made him – what's the kindest way of saying it? – Unbalanced, I suppose. I did ask him once if he really was an employee there or a patient?! He helped to look after some of society's most evil and mentally ill individuals which must be draining and take its toll on a person. Having said that, I think he would have been a happier man if he had taken a year out after leaving the hospital, then found another himself another job. He would often tell me stories of things that had happened at the hospital as well as the laughs he would have with the staff, and I think he missed being part of a workforce. The main problem he and I had was having absolutely no conversation because we had nothing to talk about which is very unhealthy. Maybe things would have been better between us if he'd had a job. Sitting in a room with him, not speaking, was hard work and I often felt tension between us, but could never understand why. Every time I picked up my I pad, he would give a big sigh which infuriated me and it is so nice now to be able to do what I want without his disapproval. Looking back, I think the main reason I married Robert was because I needed someone to cling to after my Mum's death.

All I ever wanted was to love and be loved, and at times in my life, I felt I was, but it always seemed to go downhill after a while. I hope to meet someone and fall in love again one day, a lot further down the line though, not yet. I want to be made to feel special and for a man to feel warmth and affection towards me but I'm realistic and know that unless they can look past the naughty life I've led and see the real me, it will be difficult for any man to trust me. Maybe that was another problem Robert had with me, and it made him insecure? I don't know.

Chapter 41

Before he went back to the UK he told me he wouldn't be going anywhere until I had given him 25, 000 euros from my inheritance. I was absolutely stunned and told him he could sod off and eventually he agreed to accept 15, 000. I was amazed that this man I had hoped to spend the rest of my life with had suddenly become such an arsehole. Just to keep the peace and get him out of my life, I gave him the money he wanted and asked him to sign a document I'd had drawn up which stated that he acknowledged receipt of the 15, 000 euros I had given him and that he would agree that at no time in the near or distant future would he try to take any more money from me-and he refused to sign it. He has now returned to the UK and I hope I won't see him again. He and I had an opportunity to have a lovely carefree life down here in the sun, neither of us had to work and I can't see what he had to be so miserable about. It's the kind of lifestyle many people can only dream about. Many of my friends have asked me if my daughter and I will be returning to the UK but we are happy and settled here and I intend to stay here. She is getting on well at an International school and I'm just enjoying living a peaceful life in the sun…which is what I always wanted…but I had hoped to be doing it with Robert. I believe he found it hard, at his age, having

Amy around all the time, but he knew I had her when he met me, and that she was part of the 'package'. People of our age are usually Grandparents and it is more tiring raising a child when you're older. But it was my choice to have her and I do love her. Children don't ask to be born.

I know in my heart that If Andrew hadn't messed up so badly, that he and I would have still been together because we had an arrangement that suited us both. I didn't realise he would turn out to be a pervert and lust after young girls. If that hadn't happened I think we would still be together now and I would never have left him to be with Robert. We got on well in our own funny little way. Such a shame he had to go and spoil everything with his stupid actions. He's the one person I could sit in the same room with and not feel I needed to make conversation. We just seemed comfortable together and I do miss the companionship that we had. All in all, I feel very disillusioned with men, and with Robert out the picture, I have been considering doing the escort work again. I know that at some point I will want sex again as that's just the way I am; also the money I would earn would go towards Amy's school fees, my rent and the usual bills which now fall on my shoulders. I have no desire to get involved with anyone seriously again and definitely will never live with another man. I don't want to have to answer to anybody anymore. I wonder if you, reading this, feel disgusted that I could consider going back to the 'old profession', or are you thinking that you don't blame me?!

What hurts me the most is the fact that since leaving me a few weeks ago, Robert has never apologised to me for his behaviour, nor has he shown any sign that he wants us to try again? There's been no contact at all. Sometimes when I feel low, I am tempted to send him a message but I don't know what I even want to say. And what is the point anyway? I am left feeling our relationship was a complete farce and don't think he ever really loved me at all. I really was in love with him and would never have shared him with anyone. And on top of that, as soon as he returned to England I noticed his family had all deleted me from Facebook. This was upsetting for me because they had all been out to visit us here and I got on well with them and made them welcome. I expect he told them a pack of lies and they all think I'm bad news-ok, maybe I am but I was good for him and to him. I did feel angry at the time and tempted to tell the lot of them how we actually met, but I managed to keep my cool and am glad now that I did. I know the truth and at the end of the day, that's what matters. On a lighter note, I did do something a bit naughty recently that have me a degree of satisfaction…

CHAPTER 42

I went on Robert's Hotmail account to be nosey and see what he was up to-I set up his account so knew his password. He hated the internet so things like that were left to me. The internet was a real bone of contention between us-he would say I spent too much time on it, and I would reply that maybe if we had some conversation, I wouldn't feel the need to go on it so much and chat to my friends… Anyway, I saw he'd received a couple of emails from a website encouraging him to complete his profile. This website was a dating/sex site. I managed to access his profile as, predictably, he had used the same password as his Hotmail account. On his 'profile' he described himself as a 40 year old business man, interested in meeting women for sex, friendship and possibly more. I thought to myself 'you lying piece of crap' I noticed he hadn't uploaded any photos on to his profile, so I decided to do it for him. I went on to google images, and typed in 'very old men'. Loads of pictures of toothless, gummy ancient looking men appeared so I selected six of the best, downloaded and saved them to my laptop-then uploaded them on to his profile….I wonder if he had much response to his advert?!!!!!! About three days after doing the dirty deed my phone rang. All I heard when

I answered it was a stream of verbal abuse that went on for a good 5 minutes...I just listened without trying to butt in and then cut him off, mid rant with a big smile on my face!

CHAPTER 43

When I confided in one of my close friends here recently that I might start doing the escorting again, she offered to take the naughty photos of me for my new profile. Of course, I'm well aware that I'm no spring chicken, but from experience I have learned that age and perfect looks are not important in the sex industry. I reckon I will still earn a few euros if I put my mind to it! I would only do in-calls, no car meets or out calls and I would not let the job consume my whole life, as I felt it did before. I compare the escorting part of my life to the excitement of a roller coaster ride, but without the brakes. I just couldn't stop it once it had started. It's not a nice thing to say about myself but I feel I am damaged goods. I don't believe any woman in this line of work can come away from it unscathed in some way or another, mentally or worse, physically. Many of my friends have said to me they wish they could do it but would be too scared to try it. I'm not going to encourage anyone to try escorting, but if you do, I hope my experiences will prepare you to what you could be in for! There are some funny men out there with many different needs! The most important thing I would say to anyone thinking about it, is just make sure you do what you can to stay safe. I was lucky, no one hurt me but other working girls aren't so fortunate. The moneys great but it can be a very dangerous game. And on a final note, avoid sea sponge, and just enjoy a few days rest!

Epilogue

It has been a couple of weeks since I wrote the last chapter and I just want to give you an update. I decided to put my profile back on the website I advertised on before. Amy and I are going back to the UK for a few days soon and as she is going to be staying with her Dad, I'm going to see some of my old clients who have found me on the website. It will be interesting to see if I fall back into the work easily or if, after a two year break, I find it difficult to do it all again-I doubt it, but you never know! The following emails are from familiar and some potential clients which I've received since putting my profile back on the site-

Cecil gee Hello, do you do bareback?

Steve Hi are you available to meet in Spain? Whereabouts are you?

Peter Peter here, how lovely to see back on here again! I have often hoped that you might re-appear at some point - I have very fond (and hard!) memories of our fabulous oral sessions and would love to repeat the experience again! ;-)

Slave Jon hello beautiful I've missed you are you camminng again? ive never met u couldnt get an incall with u when u were in bridport hope to rectify that

Deano Hi, my wife and I saw your profile on adult work and thought we should drop you an email. We are looking to have some fun with a bi lady. My wife has been with a lady escort before and really enjoyed it, so we would like to repeat the experience.

Are you free this Saturday at about 7:30pm for an outcall in Poole for an hour. My wife is 44 and bi and I'm 53, we are both highly sexed and need a lady to show us what we have been missing If you are free this Saturday please email back withe cost for 1 hour

James hi what's your number? I'll call to arrange meeting.

Nicknak I'd love to meet you for a session when your back. I live near Blandford in a dorset and would love to see you in that basque!! Let me know your plans.. Luv Nick

Rossy HELLO I ROSS I HAVE A CRYING FETISH I LIKE TO SEE WOMEN CRYING AND HEAR THEM WEEP WHAT WILL MAKE U CRY TEARS. CAN U CRY FOR ME
CAN YOU PLEASE REPLY

Steffan1 Bloody hell, There's a blast from the past!!!
Its Steve the Ex Policeman xxxx How are you honey, Hope you are well!

Wondered where you disappeared to. Would love to meet up when you are back x

Portland boy Hi how are you?

Don't know if you remember me but I met you twice at your house and had the privilege of emptying my balls inside you! :-)

I would love to meet you again! :-)

But won't know the dates until nearer the time.

Have you got much space??

Thanks

Liam

Xxx

Slave4u

I am an athletic, but not wimpy male submissive and I am looking to be a personal slave to a working lady.. I am genuine and very reliable and live alone on the south coast, but travel alot. I am obedient and very willing and would like to be considered by you as a personal slave.. I am prepared to be filmed if required and used in any way you choose either for domestic use or sexual use, to you or any other females.. I can offer accommodation and visits to my home and full pampering in any way you choose..

Please note I am not looking to pay fees or reiceive and have this profile purely so I have a profile to be viewed. Please don't hesitate to ask anything at all and equally please don't be offended if you are not interested....

Thank you.

Footbod Hi I have a foot fetish. Can I come and lick your feet and toes and what size feet are you? Are your feet wide or average size? Please reply.

These are just a few of the emails I've had-maybe I should take the 'slave' up on his offer!

When Amy and I return to Spain, I'm going to enjoy the summer holidays with her, then start 'work' again in September over here, and just see how it goes. During my week in England, I have also booked myself into a party at the swinging club I used to go to. The club owners were delighted to hear from me and say they can't wait to see me. I think I will be nervous going in there again after so long but I'm looking forward to seeing some familiar faces and having a laugh and a good catch up with some of them. I feel I've been through a lot one way or another in the last two years, I admit much of it is of my own making, but now it's time to brush myself off and get on with enjoying life again. I can't help wondering where I will be this time next year, and what I will be doing-we shall see!

Thank you for reading my book, I hope you've enjoyed it ☺

God Bless and take care,
Abigail xxxxxxxxx

A letter to my daughter,

Hello Lisa, I just want to let you know how much I appreciate the honesty we have between us. I hope you won't think I'm selfish for writing this book and not thinking of anyone except myself but I promise you, this is not true. The last thing I want is for you to suffer in any way because of my story. I just needed to write it, mainly because I hoped that in doing so, I would find some inner peace which would overshadow all the negative things that have gone on in my life during the last few years. If people like my book I believe you will be proud of me, just like your Nan would have been. I'm sorry I haven't been a more conventional Mum for you during the last couple of years, but whatever I am and whatever I've done, please know that I love you very much and always will

All my love,
Mum xx

Acknowledgements

I want to thank my friends, they know who they are, for helping me through the bad times and for accepting me for who I am. And to thank the men who have let me down – you have made me stronger.

NOTES

Printed in Great Britain
by Amazon